EXODUS

A SELF-STUDY GUIDE

Irving L. Jensen

MOODY PUBLISHERS
CHICAGO

©1967 by
THE MOODY BIBLE INSTITUTE
OF CHICAGO

Moody Publishers Revised Edition, 1990

All rights reserved. No part of this book may be reproduced in any form without permission in writing from the publisher, except in the case of brief quotations embodied in critical articles or reviews.

Scripture quotations, unless noted otherwise, are taken from the King James Version.

The use of selected references from various versions of the Bible in this publication does not necessarily imply publisher endorsement of the versions in their entirety.

Cover design: Ragont Design
Photography: V. Gibert Beers

ISBN: 978-0-8024-4457-8

We hope you enjoy this book from Moody Publishers. Our goal is to provide high-quality, thought-provoking books and products that connect truth to your real needs and challenges. For more information on other books and products written and produced from a biblical perspective, go to www.moodypublishers.com or write to:

Moody Publishers
820 N. LaSalle Boulevard
Chicago, IL 60610

9 10

Printed in the United States of America

Contents

Introduction

One purpose in preparing this study book on Exodus is to point out the remarkable correspondence between the experiences of God's people as recorded in Exodus and the experiences of a redeemed soul. The young convert has been kept constantly in mind as these lessons have been arranged.

The lessons of the study guide may be used either in individual Bible study or in group study. In either case, the student should follow the instructions of the section of each lesson entitled ANALYSIS *before* he reads the section COMMENTS. In other words, *most* of the student's work in the lesson is accomplished before he reads COMMENTS. The third section of each lesson, called SUMMARY, serves as both a review and a conclusion for the study.

Incorporated in this self-study guide are various helps for analyzing the Bible chapter by chapter and paragraph by paragraph. Convinced that "the pencil is one of the best eyes," the writer has also given suggestions along the way on how the student may record his analyses on paper.

When several are studying together it would be well for them to have a leader.

The following suggestions are directed especially to such leaders:

1. If any lesson seems too long for one meeting, do half the assigned work and plan to do the other half at the next meeting. Undertake no more than you can do thoroughly. The leader must first do the entire lesson himself in order to determine how and where to divide the lesson.

2. If possible, have before the class at each meeting enlarged copies (made either on cloth or paper) of the chart and map on page 63.

4

3. Insist that class members study the lesson at home and bring to the class their recorded observations, analyses, and answers to questions. Encourage the use of the pencil as a *must* for methodical, fruitful Bible study.

4. Keep reminding the members to read the assigned chapters in the Bible *first*, before they proceed with their study.

5. Have a short review of the previous work at the beginning of each meeting.

6. Have one or more members of the class tell the story of the chapter (or chapters) briefly, locating geographical places on the map when necessary.

7. In tracing the journey of the children of Israel, a black tape or ribbon could be pinned on the map at the different places as the journey progresses.

8. Insist that the members of the class think and study for themselves. Independent Bible study is most gratifying and fruitful. Teachers and students who are interested in learning more about some of the methods of firsthand analysis suggested in this study guide are referred to the book *Independent Bible Study*.[1]

9. Give the members of the class opportunity to share their thoughts and the lessons they have learned. Refuse to lecture to the class.

10. Constantly emphasize the importance of carefully looking up all scriptural references given in each lesson. Urge members of the class not to neglect this. It is true that the Bible is its best interpreter.

---

1. Irving L. Jensen (Chicago: Moody, 1963).

Lesson 1
The Book of Exodus

The study of any individual book of the sixty-six of the Bible involves the following three areas:

1. Study of the book's background
2. Survey study of the whole book
3. Analytical study of each part of the book (each part may be more or less than one chapter)

The three areas designated above should be studied in the order in which they are listed. This lesson is a guide for the first two studies; all the succeeding lessons deal mostly with the analytical studies.

I. THE BACKGROUND OF EXODUS

Concerning any book of the Bible, we should be interested in who wrote it, when it was written, what its chief theme is, and what relation it bears to the Bible as a whole. Some answers to these questions are given here your own personal survey study will provide further light.

A. Name

The second book of the Bible has been given the title *Exodus* to represent one of the main historical events of its narrative: the Israelites' exit or *departure* from Egypt (read Ex. 19:1). The English title is derived from that of the Latin Vulgate, *Exodos*, which is based on the title *Exodus* of the Greek Septuagint version.

B. Writer

Jewish tradition ascribes to Moses the first five books of the Bible. Christ explicitly ascribed the Pentateuch to Moses (Luke 24:44). As mentioned in this verse, the biblical authors divided the Old Testament into three parts—the Law, the Prophets, and the Psalms (the Psalms being representative of the large section called "Writings"). Christ frequently referred to different books as being written by Moses. For example, compare Mark 12:26 with Exodus 3:2-5; Matthew 8:3-4 with Leviticus 14:3-4; Matthew 19:7-8 with Deuteronomy 24:1-4. Also the text of Exodus itself clearly refers to Mosaic authorship (17:14; 24:4).

C. Date

Moses wrote Exodus sometime during the last half of the fifteenth century B.C. This is based on the 1445 B.C. date of the Israelites' exodus from Egypt.

D. Theme

Exodus is the book of redemption in its broad meaning. As of the beginning of the book, the descendants of Abraham are residents of Egypt, under rigorous bondage and oppression by Egypt's pharaoh. Exodus describes how God delivered Israel from that bondage by bringing them out of Egypt. But this is only the negative aspect of the large word *redemption*. Positively, God brought the Israelites into a covenant relationship with Himself, making them a "peculiar treasure" unto Himself (19:5) and giving them a law, which was to be the foundation of their national existence. This positive aspect of Israel's redemption is the theme of the last half of the book of Exodus. The redemption narrative of Exodus is thus one of the remarkable Old Testament illustrations of the great redemption wrought by Christ through Calvary.

E. Interval of Time Between Genesis and Exodus

When we open the book of Exodus we must bear in mind that many years have intervened between the events recorded in the last chapters of Genesis and the events which are now to occupy us. Also many changes have taken place. At the close of Genesis we left the chosen people of God (the descendants of Abraham through Jacob, or Israel) just a small family, consisting of Jacob's twelve sons with their wives and children, living in Egypt in the land of Goshen. Then they were the most favored people in the land. When we open Exodus, we find them grown to a great multitude; and instead of being the most favored by the peoples in Egypt, they are in bitter bondage to Egypt's rulers.

But observe God's hand. See how He is gradually bringing about His promise concerning them (Gen. 15:13-16). In Genesis, chapter 46, we saw fulfilled the first part of this prophecy, the going into Egypt. Now in Exodus we shall see the second part, the going out of Egypt, accomplished.

II. A SURVEY OF EXODUS

"Image the whole; then execute the parts." is the correct procedure for Bible study. Begin your study of Exodus by making a rapid cursory reading of the entire forty chapters in one sitting and thus gaining an overall "skyscraper view" of the book as a whole. In this beginning stage of your study do not tarry over minute details; seek to get the "feel" of the book and observe its "flow" or progression. Write down your impressions thus far, and record any key words or phrases that have stood out from the text.

Now go back to each chapter and secure from the text of each chapter a picturesque word or short phrase that will serve as a clue to a leading thought in the chapter. Record your forty chapter titles on a chart similar to the following:

RECORDING CHAPTER TITLES FOR EXODUS

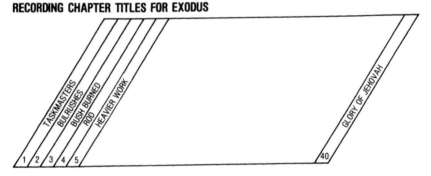

When you have done this, you will have a fair grasp of at least the large movements or groups of material in Exodus.

Referring to the text of Exodus as often as necessary, secure answers to the following questions, recording your observations on your own chart, similar to the format of the chart illustrated in this lesson.

1. Contrast the first and last chapters of Exodus. What is the state of Israel in each chapter?

_____

_____

EXODUS BOOK OF REDEMPTION

A key word: "deliver"
(2:19; 3:8; 5:23; 12:27;
18:4, 8, 9, 10)

A key expression:
"As the LORD
commanded Moses"

DELIVERANCE				WORSHIP	
				SINAI INSTRUCTIONS	
MOSES AND BURDENS OF ISRAEL	PHARAOH AND PLAGUES UPON EGYPT	RED SEA DELIVER-ANCE	WILDERNESS PROVISION	TABERNACLE PATTERN	IDOLATRY	TABERNACLE CONSTRUCTION

BONDAGE — BIRTH OF MOSES — CALL OF MOSES — "I AM THE LORD." — PLAGUES — PASSOVER — RED SEA — WILDERNESS — TEN COMMANDMENTS — LAW — GLORY OF LORD

1 2 3 4 5:1 5:22 7:14 8 9 10 11 12 13 14 15:1 15:22 17 18 19 20 21 22 23 24 25 26 27 28 29 30 31 32 33 34 35 36 37 38 39 40

S I N A I

ISRAEL IN EGYPT	ISRAEL TO SINAI	ISRAEL AT SINAI
BONDAGE AND OPPRESSION	DELIVERANCE AND PROVISION	LAW, PATTERN, AND CONSTRUCTION
GOD'S PEOPLE ENDURING BONDAGE	GOD'S GRACE REVEALED IN REDEMPTION	GOD'S GLORY MANIFESTED IN WORSHIP

FROM GROAN

TO GLORY

9

2. Make a list of the major *events* of Exodus and the major *characters*.

_____

_____

3. What about the *geography* of Exodus? Show the major areas (not individual places as such) of Exodus's geography on your chart.
4. Compare the general content of the first half of Exodus with that of the last half.

_____

_____

5. What is the main difference between the content of chapters 25–31 and that of chapters 35–40?

_____

_____

6. Name three major truths about God that appear prominent in the text of Exodus.

_____

_____

7. From your knowledge of Christ's ministry, what items of Exodus illustrate particular aspects of that ministry?

_____

_____

Having accomplished the above survey study thus far on your own, now proceed to read the remainder of this lesson as an amplification of your survey study.

A. The Structure of Exodus

Study the accompanying survey chart of the major groups of content in Exodus.

Note the following:

1. Exodus has forty chapters. Each numbered space in the above chart, represents a segment, segments usually being the length of one chapter.

2. There are, in Exodus, eight principal subjects; eight great facts around which the smaller facts group themselves; eight words by which one can hold the contents of the book in mind

10

and think through consecutively. Look at the chart and observe that these eight subjects are:

BONDAGE (1:1-22)	PASSOVER (12:1-51)
BIRTH OF MOSES (2:1-25)	RED SEA (13:1–15:21)
CALL OF MOSES (3:1–7:13)	WILDERNESS (15:22–18:27)
PLAGUES (7:14–11:10)	SINAI (19:1–40:38)

It should be noted that the last plague, as threatened in chapter 11, does not fall upon Egypt until 12:29-30, in the middle of the Passover chapter.

3. Observe that under SINAI, there are four subdivisions, viz:

a. Law, chapters 19-24

b. Tabernacle instructions, chapters 25-31

c. Idolatry, chapters 32-34

d. Tabernacle construction, chapters 35-40

4. Considered geographically, Exodus falls into three chief divisions as indicated on the chart:

a. Israel in Egypt, chapters 1-12

b. Israel to Sinai, chapters 13-18

c. Israel at Sinai, chapters 19-40

See the map on page 63, and fix in your mind this geographical divisions in Exodus.

B. Types of Christ

C. I. Scofield states: "A type is a divinely purposed illustration of some truth. It may be (1) a person (Rom. 5:14); (2) an event (1 Cor. 10:11); (3) a thing (Heb. 10:20); (4) an institution (Heb. 9:11); (5) a ceremonial (1 Cor. 5:7). Types occur most frequently in the Pentateuch, but are found, more sparingly, elsewhere. The anti-type or fulfillment of the type, is found usually in the New Testament."

Some of the great types of Christ in Exodus are:

GENERAL TYPES

1. The *Paschal Lamb.* Type of Christ our Redeemer (Ex. 12:1-28; cf. John 1:29; 1 Cor. 5:6-7; 1 Pet. 1:18-19).

2. The *Manna.* Type of Christ as the Bread of Life, come down from heaven to die "for the life of the world" (Ex. 16:1-36; cf. John 6:35, 48-51).

3. The *Rock.* (Ex. 17:5-6; cf. 1 Cor. 10:1-4).

4. The *Tabernacle* (Ex. 25:1–31:18; 35:1–40:38; cf. Heb. 9).

1. *Moses.* Type of Christ the Deliverer (Ex. 5:1; cf. Luke 4:16-21)

2. *Aaron.* Type of Christ our High Priest (Ex. 4:27; 7:1-2, 19; cf. Heb. 5:4; 9:4, 11-12, 25-26)

C. Symbolism in Exodus

The part of Israel's history recorded in Exodus presents a wonderful symbolism that many Bible readers entirely overlook, but which, if observed, makes this whole narrative a veritable treasure-house of spiritual and practical truth. Our authority for calling it symbolic or typical is found in 1 Corinthians 10:1-11.

C. I. Scofield has said of the Pentateuch: "The five books ascribed to Moses have a peculiar place in the structure of the Bible, and an order which is undeniably the order of the experience of the people of God in all ages. Genesis is the book of origins—of the beginning of life, and of ruin through sin. Its first word, 'In the beginning God,' is in striking contrast with the end, 'in a coffin in Egypt.' Exodus is the book of redemption, the first need of a ruined race. Leviticus is the book of worship and communion, the proper exercise of the redeemer. Numbers speaks of the experiences of a pilgrim people, the redeemed, passing through a hostile scene to a promised inheritance. Deuteronomy, retrospective and prospective, is a book of instruction for the redeemed about to enter that inheritance. In the Pentateuch, therefore, we have a true and logical introduction to the entire Bible; and, in type, an epitome of the divine revelation."

This symbolism is especially apparent in the book of Exodus. Israel in bondage to Pharaoh presents a picture of the human soul in bondage to Satan, and as we see Israel being delivered by God out of bondage, wandering in the wilderness, and at last reaching their promised inheritance, we behold a striking picture of the history of the individual soul.

Look at the map on page 63, and note the three geographical places: Egypt, the Wilderness, and Canaan. These three geographical places mark the three stages of Israel's journey and suggest the following three stages in the history of the redeemed soul:

1. *Egypt* stands for the world, or Satan's domain. Israel in Egypt, in bitter bondage, with death as the only outlook, exactly portrays the condition of a soul before salvation.

2. *The Wilderness* setbacks stand for the unsurrendered Christian life. Israel in the wilderness, murmuring, stumbling, wandering, longing for the things left behind, powerless and dissatisfied,

is a true picture of that experience of so many of God's children, wherein they are saved indeed from the penalty of sin but not yet from its power.

3. *Canaan* stands for the surrendered Christian life, the Spirit-filled, Spirit-controlled life, that in which God's children may have constant victory and delight. Israel in Canaan, as related in the book of Joshua, presents a picture of the soul wholly surrendered to God, filled with His Spirit, and enjoying His daily presence.

III. SUMMARY

Just as the story of Genesis proceeds from man's problem to God's solution, so Exodus opens with a nation's problem and closes with its redemption by God. The atmosphere of chapter 1 is indicated by the word *groan*, the atmosphere of chapter 40 by the word *glory*; and it is God throughout who brings about the change. His design of redemption for the descendants of Abraham, His beloved people, included the following:

1. Appointing a leader for Israel	(Moses)
2. Making its enemy impotent	(Plagues)
3. Delivering Israel from Egypt	(Red Sea)
4. Confirming the covenant relationship	(Promises)
5. Instituting a program of worship	(Law and Tabernacle)

From an overall view of Exodus one can thus see what a grand picture, graphically portrayed through history, is presented of God's redemptive ways with mankind. This overall view can only enhance the analytical studies of its parts, which is the object of your remaining studies in Exodus.

Lesson 2

Exodus 1:1–2:25

Bondage; Birth of Moses

The first step of your study should be to read carefully and prayerfully the first two chapters of Exodus. Do not neglect this. It is
of the utmost importance to become thoroughly familiar with the
subject matter first. No one is prepared to try to understand what
the Bible *means* until he knows exactly what it *says*. Read the
chapters over and over until you could close your Bible and tell
the whole story of these two chapters consecutively and accurately.

Following the typical teaching of this portion of Scripture, as
suggested in our last lesson under "Symbolism," our endeavor
will be to call attention to some of the points in which the experiences of Israel here recorded are analogous to the experiences of
a soul. Note 1 Corinthians 10:11: "Now all these things happened
unto them for ensamples: and they are written for our admonition."

Israel in bondage to Pharaoh furnishes a good type of a soul
in bondage to Satan. Israel is delivered from bondage and
brought out of Egypt in the way a human soul may be delivered
out of Satan's dominion. Indeed, the whole history of Israel's journey from Egypt to Canaan is a most remarkable type and is, at every step, almost startling in its likeness.

I. ANALYSIS

Having read the two chapters of this lesson according to the instructions given, you should begin now to record on paper some
of your observations while you try to discover the organization of
the writing of the narrative. Paragraph study will help you much in
this respect. Block out on a sheet of paper a rectangle similar to
the following chart, showing the various paragraph divisions.

14

1:1	
7	
15	
22	
2:1	BULRUSHES
11	
15	
23	
25	

PLIGHT

PROVISION
FOR
FUTURE
DELIVERANCE

PRAYER
TO GOD
HEARD

1. Choose a picturesque word out of each paragraph and record it in the top right-hand corner of the paragraph (see example for 2:1 paragraph).

2. Record within each paragraph box the key words and phrases from the biblical text.

3. Determine the main point of each paragraph.

4. Now look for groupings of paragraphs. Answer the following questions:

   a. In what sense does paragraph 1:1 stand alone?

   b. What is common to the next three paragraphs?

   c. What is common to paragraphs 2:1, 2:11, and 2:15?

   d. How is paragraph 2:23 a climax to the story?

5. Pharaoh is the "new king" of 1:8. At what point does he leave the narrative? Record this on your chart.

6. Outline on your chart Moses' life as given in chapter 2. How long was each period? (See Acts 7:17-30.)

7. How often is God referred to in these two chapters?

8. What spiritual lessons are taught here?

9. Before reading any further in this lesson, try to answer the following questions from information given by the biblical text:

a. When and why did the descendants of Abraham take up their residence in Egypt (Gen. 45:17-28; 47:1-4)?

_____

_____

b. What reason did Pharaoh give for enslaving the Hebrews (Exodus 1:8-10)?

_____

_____

c. Why do you suppose God allowed Israel to suffer under this bondage?

_____

_____

d. From which of the twelve sons of Jacob was Moses descended (Ex. 2:1; cf. 1:1-2)?

_____

e. What was the name of Moses' father? _____

mother? _____

sister? _____

brother? _____

wife? _____

father-in-law? _____

son? _____

16

II. COMMENTS

A. Bondage (1:1-22)

1. *Origin of bondage* (1:1-11). When the children of Israel first entered his territory, the king of Egypt was exceedingly pleasant (Gen. 47:1-6), and Abraham's descendants were contented and prosperous (Gen. 47:27). For a time it may have appeared to them that they had made a good move in leaving Canaan, the country that God had chosen for them, and coming to Egypt; but they soon saw their mistake, and it was not too many years before they found themselves helpless, hopeless slaves.

See the application. The person who turns from God to Satan may enjoy the pleasures of sin for a season, may be prosperous and apparently contented and happy, but sooner or later will find himself absolutely in the power of the devil, bound by habits of sin so strong that only God can break them.

2. *Effect and end of bondage* (1:11-22). Pharaoh was determined that these Hebrews should not escape from his power, for they could be made very profitable to him. So he took measures that, he believed, would effectually subjugate them. (Note: The phrase "more and mightier than we" of 1:9 probably has the intent "too numerous and too strong."[1] See how cruelly he treated them and how hard he made them work for him (vv. 11, 13, 14); and when that did not accomplish his purpose (v. 12), he did not hesitate to kill them (vv. 15, 16, 22). (Note: The phrase "every son" of 1:22 has the intent "every Hebrew son.") And all the while the Hebrews were bending their backs to the lash and to the burdens and were suffering under this bitter tyranny of Pharaoh, God had waiting for them the beautiful country of Canaan, "flowing with milk and honey," to which He was longing to bring them back if they would but remember Him and follow Him.

Pharaoh's plan and God's plan for Israel exhibit a wide difference. Pharaoh's plan for them was bondage, sorrow, poverty, and death. God's plan for them was liberty, joy, plenty, and life. A great contrast, surely. But that is just the wide difference between Satan's plan and God's plan for every human soul. "For the wages of sin is death; but the gift of God is eternal life (Rom. 6:23*a*).

3. *Purpose of the bondage.* When this horrible law of Exodus 1:22 was put into execution, and when the Hebrews realized their helplessness to resist, it must have seemed to them that the God of their fathers had forsaken them. But rather had they not forsak-

---

1. See Charles F. Pfeiffer and Everett F. Harrison, eds., *The Wycliffe Bible Commentary* (Chicago: Moody, 1962) p. 53.

en God? Although some, such as the midwives and Moses' parents, still retained faith in God, most of the Hebrews had gone off into Egyptian idolatry and Egyptian abominations, as is plain later on in the story. Now they had to feel the bitterness of their bondage, realize the consequences of sin, and be ready to turn to God before He could deliver them. Just so, a soul that has gone into sin must repent and turn from sin to God, before there can be deliverance.

While Israel slowly learned this lesson, God was getting all things ready for their departure, as we shall see in the next chapter.

B. Birth of Moses (2:1-25)

1. *Moses' parents* (2:1-10). Moses was the son of believing parents, and that is about the greatest blessing any child can have. Amram and Jochebed, Moses' father and mother (cf. Ex. 6:20), were evidently familiar with God's promises and past dealings with His people, and when Moses was born they seem to have entertained the hope that he was to be the deliverer of his people (see Heb. 11:23). Moses probably got that idea himself from his mother (Acts 7:25).

Amram and Jochebed had two other children besides Moses: Miriam, a little girl of perhaps ten or eleven years at the time of Moses' birth, and Aaron, three years old (see Ex. 7:7). The edict that every male child born should be cast into the river (the word "river" in Exodus refers to the Nile River), does not seem to have been in force at the time of Aaron's birth, as it was at the time of Moses'. But Moses' parents did not obey it. By faith in God they overcame the fear of Pharaoh (Heb. 11:23). Trust in God and in His word is ever the best cure for fear (Ps. 27:1; Rom. 8:31).

See how God rewarded Jochebed's faith. Not only was her boy preserved in that crocodile-infested Nile, but his safety was assured by the command of the king's own daughter, and soon Moses was back in his mother's arms and she was being paid Egyptian gold for doing the thing she would rather do than anything else (v. 9). What rejoicing there must have been in that Hebrew hut that night. How glad Moses' parents must have been that they had put their trust in God (read Prov. 29:25).

2. *Moses' education.* The best education that Moses received was given him by his God-fearing parents. It was at his mother's knee, where every child should learn eternal truths, that Moses learned God's promises concerning His people. How much better it was "to suffer affliction with the people of God than to enjoy the pleasures of sin for a season" (Heb. 11:24-26).

No doubt Moses, with Miriam and Aaron, listened and wondered as their father and mother related God's dealings with Abraham, Isaac, Jacob, and Joseph, and were especially thrilled at His assurance to Abraham (Gen. 15:13-16) that after four hundred years they should come out of bondage and possess that land of promise. The four hundred years were drawing to a close. God had said "in the fourth generation." These children would live to see its fulfillment. We are not told at what age Moses went into the king's palace as the son of the princess, but in Acts 7:22 we are told how he was occupied while being brought up as the Pharaoh's grandson. From this verse we gather that he was sent to the best schools of Egypt. He was "mighty in words" as a writer, and "in deeds" as a warrior. Although the scholars and magicians and idolatrous priests taught him all the wisdom of the Egyptians, the wisdom of God, which his mother had taught him as a child, was what molded his character and his career. Skeptical and infidel teachers cannot harm the boy or the girl who has had the previous schooling of thorough Christian instruction and example in his own home. Moses saw by experience the superiority of the religion of the Hebrews to that of Egypt.

See how God made the wrath of man to praise Him. All Pharaoh's wicked plans had simply resulted in preserving, educating, and preparing for the great works to which God would call him, the very deliverer which Pharaoh feared might come.

3. *Moses' choice* (read Heb. 11; Acts 7). It was the influence of his mother's teaching that caused Moses to make the wisest choice of his life, that of following God wholly. Amid all the wealth and pleasure and sin of the Egyptian court, Moses did not forget what he had learned in those early years in his father's home. There must have been an undercurrent of thought going on in his mind day after day. He could not forget that the men toiling in the brick kilns of Egypt were his brethren. He could not forget that his mother and father were slaves, and he could not forget those promises of God that "after four hundred years they shall come hither." Of course, appearances were all against the fulfillment of God's promises. It looked impossible. But God had said it, and Moses, like Abraham, believed God, and God counted it to him for righteousness. So at the age of forty he made his decision (see Heb. 11:24-26).

Humanly speaking, Moses turned his back on splendid opportunities, but see what he gained by the choice. He gave up a brilliant worldly career, but he gained a brilliant spiritual career. He gave up an earthly palace, but he gained a mansion in heaven. He gave up the perishable riches of Egypt, but he gained the eternal riches of Christ, Moses was a good judge of the true value of things (see Heb. 11:26).

In Hebrews 11:24 God tells us what activated Moses: *faith*. He had faith in God's word. He believed God would do just as He said—deliver the people from bondage and give them a glorious inheritance; and strong in faith, he was willing to fling away wealth, pleasure, position, and honor.

4. *Moses' rejection* (2:11-14). Moses, like Joseph and like Christ, came unto his own and his own received him not. Unlike Christ, he first tried in his own strength and in his own way to deliver his people (2:11-13). He supposed, as we read in Acts 7:25, "his brethren would have understood how that God, by his hand, would deliver them; but they understood not." They rejected him, and he, filled with fear, fled from Egypt and went into the land of Midian (see map, page 63). The Midianites were a nomadic tribe, roving about the lands on both sides of the Gulf of Aqaba; when Moses joined them they were on the west side—cf. 3:1, 12). Moses lived with the Midianites for forty years. He had made the mistake of running before God. It was not quite God's time, nor was it God's way to deliver Israel. "Moses had had forty years' training in Egypt; but before he was ready for God's work he must have forty years training at the back side of the desert, alone with God." This was Moses' postgraduate course.

There are three periods in Moses' life, each exactly forty years in duration. The first forty years he spent in Egypt learning all the wisdom of the Egyptians; the second forty years he spent in the land of Midian, being taught of God; the last forty years he was at the head of the nation, leading them out of bondage, through the wilderness and up to the Promised Land. The first forty years of his life Moses was learning that he was somebody. The second forty years he was learning that he was nobody, and the third forty years he was learning what God could do with a nobody.

5. *Moses' wife* (2:15-22). Moses married Zipporah, the daughter of the priest of Midian. Notice that she was a Gentile, that is, not a descendant of Jacob as Moses' mother had been (cf. 2:1). Zipporah was not a worshiper of God as far as we know. Later on, her lack of sympathy with God's ways is quite apparent.

After his marriage, Moses lived a quiet, simple shepherd's life which afforded opportunity for much meditation and direct teaching from God.

6. *Israel's prayer to God* (2:23-25). The years passed. Israel's bondage became intolerable. They sighed and groaned under their burdens. As their cry went up to God, He heard them, remembered His covenant, and in compassion concerned Himself

with them. The crucial time came for Him to call to Himself Moses, the deliverer whom he had been preparing, and to send him forth to the great task of deliverance.

How remarkable are God's ways, and how perfect His designs!

III. SUMMARY

In your own words, summarize the content of the first two chapters of Exodus, using the outline suggested in the analysis section: PLIGHT, PROVISION, and PRAYER.

Lesson 3

Call of Moses

In our last lesson, we saw Moses leaving Egypt, after his unsuccessful attempt to liberate his people, taking up his abode in the land of Midian and beginning his forty years of schooling in the wilderness. Tending sheep for his father-in-law seemed a lowly occupation compared with being a prince in Egypt, but Moses accepted his position without complaint (2:21), and his faithfulness as a shepherd was a preparation for the larger work God had for him (see Luke 16:10).

God tested Moses thoroughly for forty years in this position, and in our present lesson we see this faithful shepherd after those forty years, highly exalted of God.

It is interesting to compare the way in which God calls to service the different ones whom He has appointed to some great work. Read the story of His call to Gideon (Judges 6), Isaiah (Isa. 6), Jeremiah (Jer. 1:4-10), Ezekiel (Ezek. 1-3), Paul (Acts 9), and others. In every case there is first a vision of God, which humbles to the dust the one whom God so honors. Then there is a clear setting forth of the work that God wishes accomplished; often there is reluctance on the part of the one commanded to undertake the task; but there is always the assurance of God's presence and power, which enables him to go forward. Observe these things in the call of Moses.

I. ANALYSIS

First, read the two chapters carefully, underlining in your Bible the key words and phrases that stand out as important in the narrative. Sometimes a key statement might be as long as a verse, or even longer (e.g., 3:6).

Now draw a paragraph chart similar to the one of Lesson 2, dividing it into the paragraphs shown below:

22

3:1
7
13
19
22
4:1
10
18
27
31

Record a paragraph title (word or short phrase) in upper right-hand corner of each paragraph. Record key words and phrases within each paragraph block. Identify the main point of each paragraph; then look for groupings of paragraphs, according to similar content. Notice how the first paragraph stands off by itself, introducing the narrative, and how the last two form a fitting conclusion to the narrative. What takes place in between?

Introduction: 3:1-6	God's appearance to Moses
Main body: 3:7–4:17	. . . .
Conclusion: 4:18-26	Farewell to Midian
4:27-31	Welcome by Israelites

Study the five paragraphs of the main body. Record the four questions Moses asks God, in trying to escape the task God has commissioned him to do.

1. What does each question concern?

_____

_____

_____

2. What are God's answers in each case?

_____

_____

_____

3. Compare the total amount of space in the text devoted to God's assurances with that recording Moses' doubts. Conclusion?

_____

4. Notice the clear prophecy of 3:19-22.
5. Who is Moses' problem in paragraph 3:7-12?

_____

6. Who is Moses' problem in paragraph 3:13-18?

_____

7. Who worships in the first paragraph (3:1-6)?

_____

_____

In the last (4:27-31)?

_____

_____

8. What are some of the things Moses learned about God when He appeared to him (3:1-6)?

_____

_____

_____

9. What name does God call Himself in 3:14? What is the significance of such a name? How relevant was it to the situation of Moses and Israel?

_____

_____

_____

10. To whom did Moses and Aaron first announce deliverance?

_____

_____

_____

II. COMMENTS

A. Moses' Vision of God and His Divine Call (3:1-12)

By this vision Moses learned, first, that God is a consuming fire (v. 2). God appeared to Moses in a flame of fire, even as He had appeared on other occasions. (See Ex. 13:21-22; 19:18; Ezek. 1:27; cf. Heb. 12:29.)

Second, Moses learned something of the unspeakable majesty and holiness of God and that approach to Him must always be with reverence and awe (vv. 4-5; cf. Heb. 12:28-29, ASV*).

Third, Moses learned that the God who spoke to him was the same God in whom his own father had trusted, the same God who

*American Standard Version.

had dealt so wonderfully with and made such covenants with Moses' great ancestors—Abraham, Isaac, and Jacob (v. 6).

Fourth, Moses learned that God sees and hears and knows everything connected with His people (v. 7). No affliction, no crying, no sorrow escapes His tender watchful eye and ear, and He is ever near and ready to help the one who wants His help (see Ps. 145:18-19).

Fifth, Moses learned the threefold work that God had come down to do for Israel (v. 8). Fifteen hundred years later Christ came down to do this work for all mankind. Observe:

1. "To deliver them out of the hands of the Egyptians"—as He will deliver us from the hand of Satan and all our enemies (Luke 1:71, 74).

2. "To bring them up out of that land." God does not deliver from the *hand* of the Egyptians and then leave His people in the *land* of the Egyptians. He brings them out of the land also (2 Cor. 6:17).

3. "To bring them into a good land." God brings His people not only out of the bad but into the good. The problem with many Christians is that they have come out of the world (Egypt) but they have not come into fullness in Christ (Canaan). See Lesson 1 under "Symbolism."

B. Moses' Excuses (3:11–4:17)

God conferred upon Moses the greatest possible honor. He appointed him leader and deliverer of Israel. Although this was what Moses desired forty years before, now, in God's time, and in God's way, he feels unprepared. Notice his four excuses, and see if they are not the very excuses that we often make to God when He calls us to a work that seems too great.

All around us there are souls that are as much in the bondage of Satan as the Israelites were in bondage to Pharaoh; and it behooves every child of God to witness to lost souls, to try to lead them out of bondage into the Christian life.

This is always God's method: to save men through man (James 5:20; 2 Cor. 5:20). But personal work in soul-winning is about the hardest thing a Christian has to do until he learns the joy of it, and he is apt to make all the four excuses that Moses made. The early disciples, as soon as they found Christ, went directly out and began to urge their friends and neighbors to accept Him; but that most effective method of soul-winning has been largely lost sight of in these days, and we depend almost entirely upon the pulpit ministry for the salvation of the lost. If Christian men and women in the everyday walks of life would apply themselves to personal witnessing, Christ's church would assuredly make rapid progress.

1. *First excuse.* The first excuse Moses made is found in Exodus 3:11: "Who am I?" Moses felt personally inferior for such a holy and difficult task. When we are confronted with the personal duty to make an effort to lead the unsaved around us to Christ, we look within to our own unworthy selves, and well may any of us say, "Who am I?" But God gave an all-sufficient answer to Moses' questions: "Certainly I will be with thee." It does not matter who we are if God is with us. (Ps. 118:6; Rom. 8:31). God never sends His children on an errand alone. He promises always to be with them. (Deut. 31:6-8; Josh. 1:5-9; Isa. 41:8-10; Jer. 15:20; Matt. 28:20).

2. *Second excuse.* The next excuse was: "What shall I say unto them?" (3:13). Moses felt he had no answer or message to give to the Israelites. But when God sends His servants to speak He always gives the message, and the one He gave Moses is the one we should take to the unsaved. First, He said, "I AM (the One who is the Cause and Giver of all life and being, temporal and eternal) hath sent me unto you" (v. 14). Then God expressed His desire to lead souls out of bondage to Satan into the liberty of a land flowing with milk and honey—the life of Christ (vv. 16-17). That is the message that God would have us sound forth to the unsaved unto the uttermost parts of the earth.

3. *Third excuse.* Moses' third excuse was: "They will not believe me, not hearken unto my voice" (4:1). He felt the message would be unheeded by the Israelites and Pharaoh and would do no good. Satan would ever convince us that people will not believe when they hear the gospel proclaimed by our lips, and with this very argument he keeps thousands of lips closed. But God not only gives the message to His servants, He accompanies it with the power of the Holy Spirit. He gave Moses power, which, when exercised together with the message, convinced the Israelites that the message was from God, and they believed (vv. 30-31). And eventually Pharaoh also recognized that Moses spoke for God (12:31-32).

4. *Fourth excuse.* But Moses was as yet unwilling to undertake this great work, and in Exodus 4:10 he says: "I am not eloquent . . . I am slow of speech, and of a slow tongue." How many Christians hide behind that excuse, and when urged to go to the lost and tell them the way of salvation, insist that they are not eloquent, cannot talk easily like others, and therefore must be excused. Christians do not usually have difficulty about talking on other subjects, but when God would have them speak for Him, often they suddenly discover they are not eloquent. God does not

excuse Moses on that plea. He says (v. 12): "Now therefore go, and I will be with thy mouth, and teach thee what thou shalt say." God made our mouths, and He can make them work for Him if we will only surrender them.

It was not until God, in anger kindled against Moses, offered to use Aaron as Moses' mouthpiece, that Moses finally acceded to the instructions of God. This experience of Moses' life was far from exemplary of a life of faith. But it has been recorded for our admonition.

C. Moses' Return to Egypt (4:18-31)

As Moses journeyed from Midian to Egypt with his wife and sons, God talked with him, telling him how to proceed with the business on his arrival (vv. 20-23). Notice that God calls the people of Israel His "son," His "firstborn" (vv. 22-23).

From 4:20 we see that Moses' wife and two children started from Midian with him, but after the scene in the inn (vv. 24-26) Moses sent his wife back to her father, where she remained until Moses came with the children of Israel to Mount Sinai (cf. 18:1-6).

The action of 4:24-26, appearing in the narrative rather unexpectedly, is dramatic and intense. Moses, in obedience to the Lord, was on his way back to Egypt, but his journey was interrupted by a mortal ailment brought by God: "The Lord met him, and sought to kill him." The occasion for the judgment was Moses' sin. Moses was on his way to liberate the people of the circumcision, but he had failed to circumcise one of his own sons. Dr. James Gray says regarding 4:24-26: "The idea seems to be that some great mental or physical illness came upon Moses, which he recognized as a chastisement for the neglect of the circumcision of his son. This neglect was perhaps occasioned by his wife's aversion to the act (she not being a Hebrew and probably not appreciating the importance of the rite commanded in Gen. 17:14), who now overcame her maternal feelings sufficiently to perform it herself and thus bring relief to her husband."

God would not allow Moses to be the leader of the people and lawgiver, until he himself in his own family had observed the very first law that God gave for the nation—this token of the covenant (Gen. 17:9-14). The God of the Bible is the God who punishes disobedience (Deut. 28:15-21; 2 Kings 17:25). Moses had forgotten the very foundation sign of Israel's covenant relation to Jehovah. Before delivering Israel he was reminded that without circumcision an Israelite was cut off from the covenant. See Joshua 5:3-9.

After his wife's departure, Moses met Aaron, 4:27, and they went together into Egypt. The first move was to gather the elders of their people and deliver the glad message from God—that the time had come for the fulfillment of the promise made to Abraham and that soon they would march out of Egyptian bondage up to their long-promised inheritance.

The people believed (4:31), and we can well imagine how the word passed from lip to lip and from house to house, and how every heart was aglow with the hope of deliverance. The chapter ends on a solemn note, a harbinger of good things to come: "then they bowed their heads and worshipped."

III. SUMMARY

By way of a summary of these chapters of Exodus, focus your attention on the tremendous statement made by God in identifying Himself: "I AM" (3:14). Review in your mind the relationship of God as "I AM" to the various situations of these chapters. Then recall the many times Christ identified Himself in the gospels with such words as'

"I am the good shepherd" (John 10:11*a*).

"I am the light of the world" (John 8:12; 9:5).

"I am the vine" (John 15:5*a*).

That name "I AM" is like a blank check, which God gives the believer and lets him fill in whatever he truly needs. If he needs food, "I am that bread of life" (John 6:48). If he needs protection, "I am the good shepherd." If the way is dark, "I am the way, the truth, and the life" (John 14:6). How many Christians live like beggars spiritually, because they do not fully and consciously partake of Christ.

Lesson 4

The Authority of Pharaoh and the Authority of God

Moses' and Aaron's message to the people of Israel had been so promptly and warmly believed, and had brought such evident results, that no doubt they were greatly encouraged to take the next step, that of interviewing Pharaoh. God had prepared them, however, for a harsh reception from him. The ensuing action was over the issue of authority: Who has final authority, Pharaoh or God? This is where the story of this lesson begins.

I. ANALYSIS

Read 5:1–7:13 in one sitting. Before reading, mark your Bible so as to begin new paragraphs at the following locations: 5:1, 10, 15, 22; 6:9, 14, 28; 7:8. Follow the procedures of study suggested in the previous lessons, recording your paragraph analysis as shown on the accompanying chart.

1. Whose authority is prominent in the first three paragraphs? Record on your chart.

2. Whose authority is prominent in the remainder of the paragraphs?

_____

_____

3. Whose problem is described in the first three paragraphs?

_____

_____

Whose problem in the section 6:9–7:7?

_____

INCREASED BURDENS	5:1 10 15	
GREAT PROMISES	22 I AM JEHOVAH	This is the key paragraph of this lesson. Study it thoroughly.
FINAL CHARGES	6:9 14 28	
FIRST SIGN	7:8 13	

4. Note Pharaoh's question, "Who?" of 5:2 and Moses' question, "Why?" (wherefore) of 5:22. This is a pivotal point in the experiences of Israel and Pharaoh. Pharaoh's *oppression* of Israel and God's *preservation* of Israel have been countering each other since the first chapters of Exodus, and even growing in intensity. The outcome of it all will be salvation for Israel and judgment for Pharaoh. Study the diagram on the next page as a survey of these chapters of Exodus.

5. Study the paragraph 5:22–6:8 by observing the occurrences of the three phrases "I am," "I have," and "I will." What does each phrase teach about God?

_____

_____

_____

31

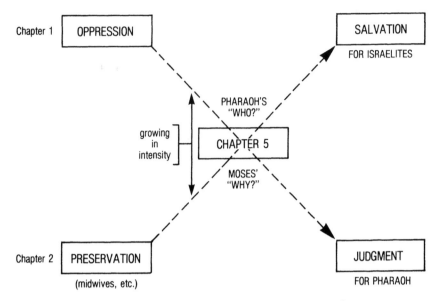

6. Study the names of God in the paragraph just cited.

6:2 "I am Jehovah (Lord)."

6:3a "And I appeared... by the name of God Almighty (El Shaddai)."

6:3b "By my name JEHOVAH was I not known to them."

Notice the strong word *covenant* in verses 4 and 5. It is one thing to make a covenant and another thing to fulfill that covenant. In view of the prominence of the phrase "I will," study the context of this paragraph by interpreting the name JEHOVAH to signify "fulfiller of the covenant."

7. Notice in 6:28–7:7 that Pharaoh's intense hardening is God's occasion to deliver Israel by "great judgments."

8. Compare the Pharaoh of the first paragraph with the Pharaoh of the last. (Pharaoh rejects the message; Pharaoh rejects a sign.)

_____

_____

_____

9. Why do you think God allowed the Israelites to get into the desperate straits as described in these chapters?

_____

_____

_____

10. List ten vital spiritual lessons you have learned from this account of Exodus.

_____

_____

_____

_____

_____

II. COMMENTS

A. Pharaoh Increases Israel's Bondage

Note the attitude that Pharaoh took from the very first, one of contempt and defiance of God (5:1-2). He asked, "Who is the Lord?"—this God who would dare to send a command to him, the great Pharaoh! He said he did not know this God, neither would he obey Him. This idea of obedience is what troubled Pharaoh. He would bend his stubborn will to no one. Even after the brothers had explained matters to him (v. 3) he would not listen to the proposition, and laid even heavier burdens upon the already overburdened Israelites, thinking that by giving them so much work he would drive all hopes of freedom from their minds. Of course, the request for a religious holiday, which Moses and Aaron made of Pharaoh, did not set forth *all* that God intended; but, as another has put it, God was under no obligation to reveal to Pharaoh all His plan, and the request was put in the most favorable light possible, so that Pharaoh would have no reasonable excuse for not granting it.

Pharaoh was the first man on record in the Bible who boasted of being an agnostic. The world is full of men today who, by their conduct, if not by their words, are crying, "Who is Jehovah that I should obey His voice? I know not the Lord." Pharaoh was soon to truly learn who the Lord was.

The first results of Moses' and Aaron's demand that Pharaoh let God's people go was the increase of their burdens and afflictions (5:6-14). Read 5:9 and note that Pharaoh spoke of God's words as "vain words" or "lying words." He was not the only one who dared thus to speak (see 2 Kings 18:20; Jer. 43:1-2). Not a few in those days regarded God's word in that light. However, all will someday find out, as did Pharaoh, that all God's words are true. Even Moses' faith seemed to have failed, and he dared to complain against God (5:22-23).

The people were now at the end of self-sufficiency. Moses and Aaron could not help them; Pharaoh would not help them; and they were powerless to help themselves. If help was to be had, it had to come from God. Just then, when they had given up hope through any other source, was the time for God to step in and save them. Notice how chapter 6 begins: "Then [when all had despaired of other means of salvation] the Lord said unto Moses, Now shalt thou see what I will do." And the rest of the chapter is an exhibition of what God did for His people. They did nothing to deliver themselves from Egypt, nor could they, beyond believing and obeying what God told them. God did it all. He devised the blood plan (Passover) by which they escaped death. He compelled Pharaoh to let them go and led them out of his domain into their inheritance.

How true a picture all this is of the soul's deliverance from Satan's bondage! When we have come to the point where we despair of deliverance by any but God, then, and only then, can God step in and give us freedom. We do not one thing to save ourselves except believe and obey what God tells us. God does it all. He devises the blood plan (redemption) whereby we escape death; He breaks Satan's power; and He leads us up out of the enemy's domain into our inheritance in Christ.

B. God's Answer to Moses' First Prayer

In 5:22 we saw Moses, in his discouragement and despair, going to God (the very best place a discouraged soul can go); and in chapter 6 we see God meeting him with assurances and promises. Read verses 1-13 and observe:

1. *First.* God contrasted His strength with that of Pharaoh. Pharaoh fancied himself mighty, and the Israelites were greatly impressed by his power, but he was a mere weakling as against God. God showed Moses that, mighty as Pharaoh was, God was *almighty*. Pharaoh had declared that he would not let Israel go; but God said He would compel Pharaoh to let the people go, and Pharaoh would be so anxious to have them depart that he would drive them out "with a strong hand" (v. 1).

2. *Second.* Then God showed Moses (vv. 3-5) that the redemption of Israel from Egyptian bondage was absolutely sure of accomplishment because it rested on the immutable, unconditional promises of God.

3. *Third.* God also told Moses (vv. 2-3) that although He had revealed Himself to Abraham, Isaac, and Jacob as the all-powerful God (El Shaddai), they had not known Him as His character of *Redeemer* in which He was now about to show Himself to Israel. JE-

HOVAH is distinctly the redemptive name of God as He fulfills the ultimate purpose of the covenant.

4. *Fourth*. Then God made a sevenfold promise, beginning each promise with "I will." Notice the seven "I wills" in 6:6-8 enclosed in a parenthesis of "I am the Lord." At the end of the book of Joshua, we see the last of all these promises of God fulfilled.

This interview with God seemed to strengthen Moses' faith, though he became quickly discouraged again when the people refused to listen (6:9-12).

The last of chapter 6 gives the names of the leaders among the descendants of the first three sons of Jacob (cf. Ex. 1:1-2), citing particularly the descendants of Levi, because Moses and Aaron were of the house of Levi. The list confirms their relationship to Israel as God's accredited leaders.

C. Contest with Pharaoh

At 7:8 begins the first confrontation of Moses and Aaron with Pharaoh involving the miraculous signs that they were to perform, attesting that they were sent by God. Before studying the series of plagues brought upon the Egyptians, consider the following truths related to the overall situation:

1. *God's love and mercy*. In studying God's dealings with Pharaoh and his people, and the sending of the plagues upon Egypt, do not overlook the love and mercy of God. Many people see only God's power and judgment; but surely His mercy and love are just as clearly manifested. Think for a moment. The attitude which Pharaoh had taken before God was one of impertinent defiance (5:2). If God had wished merely to exhibit His power and judgment, He could have instantly slain Pharaoh and every Egyptian. But instead, He went to work patiently to prove to Pharaoh and his people that the things they were worshiping were nothings, and that He alone was worthy of their adoration. Only an exhibition of power would convince them of His superiority, so He showed by the plagues what a powerful God the Hebrews had.

It would seem as if God determined to effectually answer the question that Pharaoh asked when he said, "Who is the Lord?" and to remove the ignorance of which Pharaoh complained when he said, "I know not the Lord." By the time the ten plagues were over, Pharaoh knew perfectly well who the Lord was, and that He was more powerful than all the gods of Egypt combined. And so, one after the other the plagues were brought upon Egypt, like strokes of God's rod, growing more and more severe as Pharaoh refused to yield.

2. *God's superior power.* Notice that before God sent any of the plagues He gave Pharaoh ample proof of His power in the miracle of 7:8-10, for even though Pharaoh's magicians imitated the miracle "with their enchantments" (7:11), the superior power of God was sown in that "Aaron's rod swallowed up their rods" (7:12). God gave this exhibition of His power in response to Pharaoh's request (7:8-9). The plagues also had as one of their purposes to prove to Pharaoh that God is the Lord. But Pharaoh would not be convinced.

3. *Ability of magicians.* As noted above, Pharaoh's magicians were able in some manner to imitate the miracle of Aaron's rod turning into a serpent. There are two possible explantions:

a. There was some form of trickery, such as using a snake that previously had been trained to remain rigid like a stick.

b. This was a manifestation of Satanic power, granted to Satan's ministers trafficking in the demon realm.

Either one of these explanations also accounts for the magicians' imitations in the blood and frog plagues. In all the cases, however, it was made clear to Pharaoh that the imitations of the magicians were not of the miraculous character of the phenomena attending Moses' and Aaron's rod.

4. *The hardening of Pharaoh's heart.* This seems to be a stumbling block to many people. But it must be remembered that the messages and judgments of God were the occasion rather than the cause of the hardening. In 7:3 God said, "I will harden Pharaoh's heart" (cf. 9:12), but only in the sense that God's words and ways would be the occasion for that hardening, or, stated another way, God hardens only those who choose to harden themselves. That Pharaoh himself was responsible for his hardened heart is clearly taught by the phrase "Pharaoh's heart is hardened, he refuseth . . ." (7:14). Compare also such verses as:

7:13 "Pharaoh's heart was hardened" (ASV; the KJV rendering is inaccurate.)

8:15 "Pharaoh . . . hardened his heart."

8:19 "Pharaoh's heart was hardened."

Dr. James Gray says regarding this: "Such passages must be interpreted in the light of the Divine character and the Holy Scriptures taken as a whole; and we know therefrom that God never deals unjustly or arbitrarily with His creatures, whose own free actings are always the cause of their downfall and punishment." (Cf. 2 Thess. 2:10-12.)

Consider the illustration of the sun shining on two different materials such as clay and wax. The heat melts the wax but hardens the clay. There is no difference in the rays, but rather in the materials on which they shine. The very judgments and messages that hardened Pharaoh's heart melted the hearts of some of his servants. So it is with the gospel; when presented to those who reject it, it serves only to make their hearts harder; yet it melts the hearts of those who are ready to receive it. God (or God's messages and judgments) hardened Pharaoh's heart, so we might say the gospel hardens hearts. But this only occurs when it is rejected. Substituting the words "God's messages and judgments" for the words "the Lord" in such passages as 9:12, will bring out this thought.

It is sometimes argued that since God told Moses, before he went to Egypt, that He (His messages and judgments) would harden Pharaoh's heart, therefore Pharaoh was not responsible. The fact that God told Moses this did not compel, but simply foretold Pharaoh's attitude. God would not be God if He did not know all things from the beginning; but His knowledge does not compel action.

III. SUMMARY

The story of these chapters of Exodus may be summarized by the following outline:
    A. Authority of Pharaoh (5:1-21)
    B. Person and work of God (5:22–6:8)
    C. Authority of God (6:9–7:13)
From your own personal study, fill in the items of the narrative that suggest the above outline.

Lesson 5

The Plagues

The plagues that God sent against Pharaoh and the Egyptians occupy a comparatively large space in the narrative of Exodus (note also the many chapters of Revelation describing the three series of judgments). Why did God extend the punishment? It surely was not that He delighted to see His creatures suffer. One answer to the question is that He would impress upon all people, by repetition and intensification, the truth of His absolute authority and inviolable holiness. Another answer is that He is longsuffering in His desire to have men turn their hearts to Him and thus extends the time for repentance unto salvation. As you study the plagues of Exodus, look for more than just the judgment aspect, and you will learn much about God's love for man.

It is a good thing to read straight through at one sitting the entire account of these judgments upon Egypt (7:14–11:10; 12:29-36) to familiarize yourself with the whole story. Imagine yourself passing through the experiences. Think how it would be now if similar plagues should come upon your country.

I. ANALYSIS

Now return to the text of Exodus, and underline key words and phrases. Note also phrases that repeat themselves from plague to plague. Keep in mind that repetition is a literary device used for emphasis.

Study the chart that appears with this lesson. As you read each plague, mark with an X or record word observations in the appropriate boxes describing each plague. Then answer the following questions:

THE TEN PLAGUES OF EGYPT

DESCRIPTION	1 BLOOD 7:14-25	2 FROGS 8:1-15	3 LICE 8:16-19	4 FLIES 8:20-32	5 MURRAIN 9:1-7	6 BOILS 9:8-12	7 HAIL 9:13-35	8 LOCUSTS 10:1-20	9 DARKNESS 10:21-29	10 DEATH 11:1-10 12:29-36
WARNING GIVEN IN THE MORNING										
PLAGUE NOT ANNOUNCED										
REALM AFFECTED										
NATURE OF PLAGUE										
ISRAELITES SHIELDED										
MAGICIANS IMITATE										
CONFESSION BY EGYPTIANS										
PHARAOH PROMISES LIBERTY										
PHARAOH BREAKS PROMISE										
RELATION OF EGYPTIAN GODS	NILE RIVER: main object of worship	FROG: symbol of fertility		FLIES: (Scarab beetle?) symbol of sun-god	CATTLE: ram, goat, bull: sacred				DARKNESS: ra, sun-god	

"The LORD hardened the heart of Pharaoh" 9:12

1. In what sense does the last plague stand alone?

_____

What is the reason for the delay of its fulfillment in the Exodus story?

_____

2. Show how the other nine plagues appear to fall into groups of three.

_____

_____

_____

3. Show how the plagues increased in intensity.

_____

_____

_____

4. Some plagues were warned of beforehand. Why?

_____

Some plagues were not warned of beforehand. Why not?

_____

5. How was the miraculous element of the plagues emphasized by the shielding of the Israelites?

_____

By the part played by the magicians?

_____

By the time announcements?

_____

By the undoing of the plagues?

_____

_____

6. To what extent did the Egyptians, including Pharaoh and the magicians, acknowledge God? Was there ever any real spirit of repentance in Pharaoh?

_____

_____

7. Study the compromises made by Pharaoh.

8. Notice from 9:12 that God hardened Pharaoh's heart. Consider the possibility that God effected this knowing that any surrender on Pharaoh's part from this time on would not be a heart decision but merely an outburst of physical and mental exhaustion. At the same time recognize the reality of the commands that followed (e.g., 9:13; 10:3).

9. What was the underlying purpose of God in the plagues?

_____

_____

10. List five other spiritual lessons taught by these chapters.

_____

_____

_____

_____

_____

_____

II. COMMENTS

A. Pharaoh's Stubborness

Pharaoh refused to bend his will to God. His magicians and servants were convinced of God's power, and some of them acted upon the light they received and urged Pharaoh to do so (8:19; 9:20; 10:7), but Pharaoh persistently steeled himself against the light. Again and again he seemed on the point of yielding, and then his heart would harden and he would refuse to obey. There is no ice so hard as that which melts by day and freezes by night.

Twice Pharaoh confessed himself a sinner (9:27; 10:16), and once he asked Moses to forgive him for the way he had treated him (10:17), but he did not call upon _God_ to forgive him, and he refused to turn from his sin. It was not that Pharaoh did not _know_ that he was a sinner and that God was righteous. The trouble was not with Pharaoh's *head* but with his *heart*. There are many who know perfectly well that they are sinners and are convinced of the righteousness of God, but, like Pharaoh, they refused to forsake their sin and call upon God for forgiveness, and they therefore perish. "For whosoever shall call upon the name of the Lord shall be saved" (Rom. 10:13).

B. The Ten Plagues

It is interesting to observe that some of the plagues were evidently directed against objects of Egyptian worship. For example, the Nile was the patron goddess of the Egyptians; but its waters were turned into blood, showing that the God of the Hebrews was superior in power to that idol. One of their gods was represented by a frog's head; the scarab beetle, which may have been the insect of the fourth plague, was the symbol of their sun-god, Ra; the ram, the goat, and the bull, all objects of the fifth plague, were sacred animals. The Egyptians worshiped the god of nature, and the fearful hailstorm proved that the God of the Hebrews had under His control the natural elements. They idolized Ra, god of the sun, which was turned into darkness by the true God.

It was as if God had gone throughout Egypt and struck a blow at idols being worshiped, to show how powerless—even disastrous—were the things in which the Egyptians were putting their trust. Furthermore, God wanted to convince not only the Egyptians, but the Israelites as well, that He alone was worthy of worship (see 10:1-2).

C. God's Children Protected

Notice that only the first three plagues touched the children of Israel, God allowing none of the others to occur in the land of Goshen where the Hebrews dwelt (8:22; 9:6-7, 25-26; 10:4-6, 23; 11:7).

D. Growing Severity

Notice the growing severity of the judgments. The first four plagues touched only the comfort and health of the people. The fifth plague touched their property (death to cattle in the field). The sixth plague brought intense physical pain. The seventh and eighth plagues affected more of the Egyptians' property (servants, cattle, herbs, trees). The ninth plague of thick darkness induced mental frustration and turmoil, whereas the final plague brought death to the home. (Note: More on this last plague will be studied in the next lesson.)

E. Pharaoh's Attempts at Compromise

The whole land of Egypt was trembling under the strokes of divine judgment, and yet Pharaoh refused to let the people go. Several times he seemed just on the point of letting them go, and several times he tried to compromise with Moses.

We have seen how the story of Exodus presents a remarkable symbolism to be observed. Constantly keep in mind that at every major step of Israel's journey may be seen a likeness to the history of the soul. The people's condition before coming out of bondage, the manner in which they were delivered, and all the occurrences along the way show this remarkable correspondence.

Here was a nation in bitter bondage to Pharaoh; the only outlook was death. Messengers from God brought the glad news that there was an inheritance beyond, to which He would bring them. They believed and desired to go. Pharaoh refused, and there was a struggle. When at last Pharaoh, by the mighty power of God, was compelled to let them go, he tried to make them compromise. That is just the experience of a human soul. Before I was saved I was in bitter bondage to Satan, my only outlook being eternal death. But messengers from God came and told me there was an inheritance above into which God wished to lead me. I believed and desired to go. Satan objected, and there was a struggle; and when he was compelled to release me, he tried to make compromises. This is a pattern for the ways of Satan.

Notice Pharaoh's four subtle attempts to compromise with Moses and see if they are not the very attempts Satan makes to compromise with Christians; unfortunately, many yield to one or more of them.

1. *First attempt.* In Exodus 8:25 we read, "Go ye, sacrifice to your God in the land." This was the first concession of any kind that Pharaoh made. He allowed them to worship God but objected to their going out of Egypt. In other words he said to them, "You can worship your God just as well here in Egypt. There is no need for you to separate yourselves from us and go to the other side of the Red Sea. Worship your God if you must; but stay with us."

This is the first compromise Satan tries to make with one determined to live for God. He objects to separation from sin and the world and would try to convince us we can worship God just as well "in the land" without coming out and being separate, without publicly confessing Christ before the world and taking our stand on God's side. Moses was too clever to be deceived by any such talk, and we ought also so to be, in the light of 2 Corinthians 6:14-17; Matthew 10:32-33; and Galatians 1:4.

2. *Second attempt.* The second attempt at compromise that Pharaoh made is recorded in 8:28, "Only ye shall not go very far away." Pharaoh must have realized by this time how powerless he was before Israel's God. But he tried further compromise with the people. He saw he could not prevent their leaving his domain. Moses was firm on that point; but Pharaoh would not have them go very far away! Of course not. He wanted them to stay near the border of Egypt, separated only by that narrow strip of water, the arm of the Red Sea, so that he could lure them back and again get them under his control.

Even so Satan would ever have God's people maintain a borderline position, taking their stand as God's people, yet living so nearly like the unsaved that it takes great wisdom to determine on which side they belong. God's or the devil's. Such a position suits Satan's purposes exactly; it renders the individual of no use in God's cause, and his example prevents others from becoming Christians. But God would have us get just as far away from the old life as possible, up into the Spirit-filled life where we walk with Him, becoming so occupied with our inheritance in Christ and our work for Him that Old Egypt and its ways will have no attraction for us.

In this second proposal Pharaoh virtually said to Moses, "Announce yourself a follower of God, if you must, but don't be too unworldly. Don't go very far away from the world."

3. *Third attempt.* Pharaoh's third attempt, recorded in 10:8-11, was to get Moses to consent to leave the children behind, with only the men going off to worship. Pharaoh wanted to keep a hold on the young people; hence he tried to convince Moses that this worshiping God in the wilderness, so far from Egypt, was only suitable for adults.

Compare Pharaoh's reasoning with that of Satan today. Satan argues, in effect, that a separated, consecrated life is well enough perhaps for *old* people, but the young people should be left in the world to enjoy themselves and sow their wild oats, and then when they get old they should attend to spiritual things. But young as well as old need God. Furthermore the church needs consecrated young people as well as older ones, and nothing is so encouraging as to see young people in these perilous days coming out and taking a firm stand for the separated, consecrated life.

4. *Fourth attempt.* Pharaoh's last desperate attempt at compromise is recorded in 10:24. "Only let your flocks and your herds

be stayed." He still wanted to keep control of the property! So does Satan. When he fails at ever other point, he would still have a hand in our temporal affairs and have our business conducted according to his principles, so as to injure our testimony for God. Those who are tempted along this line should frequently read Matthew 16:25-26 and Luke 18:18-25. Moses' courage to give not an inch to Pharaoh is magnificent. He said they would not leave a hoof in Egypt. They would need to worship God with their substance, so they had to take everything they possessed and consecrate it to the Lord. Such worship would involve animal sacrifices ("that we may sacrifice unto the Lord our God," 10:25), and it would also involve serving God in their daily living ("for thereof must we take to serve the Lord our God" 10:26). This determination to serve God in the new land was indelibly impressed upon Moses' heart and mind by God's repeated command to Pharaoh, a phrase that surely must be a key phrase of this section of Exodus:

"Let my people go, *that they may serve me*" (7:16; 8:1, 20; 9:1, 13; 10:3).

As Christians we must not overlook this blessed and important truth that we are *saved to serve.*

Moses was Israel's great leader and deliverer, and in this respect he typified Christ, who is our great Leader and Deliverer. Just as Moses withstood every temptation of Pharaoh and delivered from bondage and the power of Pharaoh all who followed him, so Christ withstood every temptation of Satan, and delivers from bondage and the power of Satan all who follow Him.

F. The Final Plague

An end of the plagues was inevitable. God's power had been forcefully demonstrated to all; Pharaoh's heart was of stone; and it was time for Israel to be delivered, so that the people might serve the Lord. When the midnight hour struck, as Pharaoh had been forewarned, God smote all the firstborn of the Egyptians, and then for the first time Pharaoh unconditionally released the Israelites: "Go, serve the Lord, as ye have said" (12:31). Not only were the Israelites allowed to depart in peace, they left Egypt laden with costly jewels and raiment of the Egyptians, for "the Lord gave the people favour in the sight of the Egyptians" (12:36). (Note: the King James word *borrow* of 3:22 and 12:35 is correctly translated "ask," and the King James word *lent* of 12:36 is correctly translated "granted.")

III. SUMMARY

The Exodus story of the plagues is essentially the story of a context between God and Pharaoh. The prize is the people of Israel. God is the righteous, active Challenger who originates the action and is always the winner; Pharaoh is the evil, passive subject whose refusals always make him the loser. Moses, as God's messenger, comes through the experience with a faith confirmed, exhilarated, and strengthened. Israel, God's people, witness the miracles of their protection from harm, and experience the final great miracle of their deliverance from their oppressor. The next chapters of Exodus have more to say about this deliverance.

Lesson 6

The Passover

The tenth plague of death upon all Egypt's firstborn is involved with one of the greatest experiences of Israel, and surely the greatest memorial feast—the Passover. The same event was judgment for Egypt and redemption for Israel. There is another very significant dual relationship bound up in the event of the Passover: at midnight the Israelites were to be *delivered* from the bondage of Egypt (this related to the past), but at the same time they were to be initiated into a new future relationship with God, being *adopted* as He elect people (read 6:6-7) for this dual significance). When the Passover is seen in that light, one can well understand the design of God in assigning crisis, pathos, awe, pageantry, and memorial status to the events beginning at the stroke of midnight, as intended for Israel's edification.

For the Christian the significance of the Passover cannot be overlooked, for the Lamb is the preeminent type of Christ in His atoning work. With these things in mind you should come to chapter 12 of Exodus with great anticipation and matched diligence.

I. ANALYSIS

Up until now the individual lessons of this study guide have covered more than one chapter in the biblical text. The subject of this present lesson is only one chapter, partly because of the importance of the chapter as a whole.

First read chapter 12 of Exodus a few times until you are thoroughly familiar with the account. Nothing can take the place of this. The Bible is wonderfully self-interpretive. Much in a passage will be clearly comprehended if the text is read carefully, repeatedly, and prayerfully.

Now draw an analysis rectangle on a piece of paper (8 1/2" x 11") as suggested in the earlier lessons, making the following paragraph divisions: 12:1, 11, 15, 21, 29, 37, 43. If your Bible does not show some of these divisions, mark your Bible accordingly. Follow the analysis procedures outlined in the early lessons, and record your observations. Notice how groupings of paragraphs are identified in the following chart.

EXODUS 12: 1-51

1	LAMB
11	HASTE
15	UNLEAVENED
21	ELDERS
29	SMOTE
37	600,000
43	STRANGER
51	

1. If you followed the above arrangement, what would you say is common to the first four paragraphs?

_____

_____

To the next two?

What is the last paragraph about?

2. Now record four words or phrases, one for each of the first four paragraphs.

How does the second paragraph (vv. 11-14) differ from the first paragraph?

3. The instructions of verses 15-20 were apparently not given for the immediate occasion of Israel's departure, but for the future observances of this festival of unleavened bread. What was the purpose of God in associating this feast with the Passover?

How might the event of verse 39 be remembered by the generations that followed, who observed the Feast of Unleavened Bread? What might have been the spiritual purpose of the long period of seven days?

4. Why were the people given instructions to observe the Passover feast *"forever"*?

5. Notice the phrase "mixed multitude" of the paragraph (37-42).

What spiritual truth is taught by the regulation of verse 49?

6. From verses 1-20 reconstruct a calendar of events for Israel in this "beginning of months." Record on a horizontal line:

DAY				
1	2	3	4	etc.

7. What phrases from this chapter indicate that the actual *exodus* from Egypt was a memorable event for Israel?

_____

_____

8. What are some of the impressive implications of the number of Israelites journeying from Egypt and of the number of years the nation had made its residence in Egypt? What may be learned of God from this?

_____

_____

Now consider the spiritual truths derived from the Passover lamb. From your previous knowledge of the New Testament teaching about Christ as the sacrificial Lamb, answer the following:
9. What are some of the points in which the Passover lamb typifies Christ?

_____

_____

_____

10. What Christian memorial corresponds to the Passover feast which God commanded the Israelites to observe?

_____

_____

11. What did the Israelites do besides *believe* God that night?

_____

_____

12. From what did the Israelites begin to date their sacred year? (cf. Num. 1:1). What is the Christian application?

_____

_____

13. Note the references to *obedience to God* in chapter 12.

II. COMMENTS

Chapter 12 brings us to the last night God's people spent in Egypt. Pharaoh had stubbornly and repeatedly refused to let the people go; and now God, as He had threatened at the first (see Ex. 4:22-23), was going to bring one last judgment upon the land. The death angel was to pass over Egypt, and the firstborn in every home was to die. But God devised a plan whereby all Israelites who believed and acted upon it were saved from this physical death. This plan, the Passover, is an exact type of the plan which God has devised for the world, the plan of redemption whereby all who believe and act upon it are saved from spiritual death. That this Passover lamb points to Christ is clearly taught by 1 Corinthians 5:7, and the type is full of meaning as we shall see.

Let us fix carefully in mind just what took place on that night and see how exact the type is in every detail.

The people were instructed to take a *lamb*; no other animal would do. The lamb had to be without spot or blemish and in its first year—the prime of its existence. This innocent lamb was to be slain, and with a bunch of hyssop the blood was to be put on "the lintel and the two side posts" of each house—not on the threshold, because the precious blood was not to be trampled upon.

When the death angel came by at midnight, he did not stop to inquire what kind of people lived within the house—old or young, rich or poor, good or bad. He simply ascertained if the blood had been applied, and if so he passed on. Those within these houses were saved from death—not because of their righteousness, but because they were trusting in the blood. At every house where the blood was not found, the death angel went in and slew the firstborn.

At midnight a great cry was heard throughout the land of Egypt. Pharaoh called for Moses and Aaron and not only gave full and free consent to the people's leaving but urged them to do so, and the Egyptians echoed his request. There was no attempt at compromise now. All Egypt was thoroughly aroused. The one desire was to get the Hebrews out of the land with all haste, and at any cost, that the Egyptians might not be "all dead men." The Egyptians refused nothing that was asked of them; and so, the Hebrews loaded with jewels of silver, jewels of gold, and raiment, left the land that Jacob and his sons had entered 430 years previously.

Consider now the following important truths of this chapter of Exodus.

1. The blood on the doorpost signified that the people within that house had believed and accepted God's way of salvation from death—they were trusting in the blood, and nothing else. Read verse 13, and notice that it does not read: "When I see *how righteous* you are, I will pass over you." Instead it reads: "When I see *the blood*, I will pass over you." So it was the blood of the lamb that saved the Israelites from death; and it is the blood of Christ alone that saves us from death. (Read Col. 1:20; Rom. 3:24-25; 5:9; Matt. 26:28; Rev. 1:5; 1 Pet. 1:18-19.) If some Israelite should have rationalized, "I see no need of slaying the lamb, I will just fasten it to my door and imitate its meekness and purity," the firstborn in that house would have perished that night. It was on the cross that Jesus made atonement (1 Pet. 2:24; Gal. 3:13).

2. *God's* seeing the blood gave the Israelites deliverance, and *their* seeing it gave them *assurance*, for when they saw it they knew they were safe (Ex. 12:13). If the Israelites had questioned their security after applying the blood, they would have been doubting God's word. Similarly if we doubt our security and are really trusting in the blood of Christ, we are doubting God's word. Any one behind the blood was safe and no one outside the blood was safe, no matter how good he might have been nor how strong he might have felt.

3. See how the Israelites were occupied behind those blood-stained doors while death and judgment raged all around them. The New Testament tells us that we should be occupied in this manner when safe behind the blood of Christ. Notice that they were not sleeping or entertaining themselves in foolish revelry, as too many of God's children are doing today. Instead they were awake, alert, and obedient. They were feeding upon the lamb, bitter herbs, and unleavened bread. They had their loins girded, shoes on their feet, and staff in hand, ready to go when and where God commanded. So we, when saved by the blood, are to feed upon Christ whose blood has saved us from death, constantly remembering what this salvation has cost Him (suggested by the bitter herbs), separated from all manner of evil (of which leaven is a type), and maintaining the attitude of pilgrims and strangers ready to go when and where God commands.

4. God said this day was to be kept for a memorial when they came into the land (12:25-27; cf. vv. 14, 42). Christians also have a memorial ordinance to observe, commemorating the death of Jesus. This is the Lord's Supper, or the Communion service. We are to thus remember the Lord's death regularly, for as often as we eat

52

the element of bread and drink of the cup we proclaim the Lord's death until He comes again (read Luke 22:19-20; 1 Cor. 11:23-29).

5. Notice (vv. 1-2) that God told Moses that this month was to be the first month of the year to them. Their civil year was to continue unchanged, beginning in the autumn. But now they were to begin to mark time according to a new calendar, observing their relationship to God as His people, according to *sacred* years. And this month, Abib (March-April), was to be the beginning of months for that sacred year (cf. 13:4).

This Passover night was thus the beginning of the life of Israel as a nation born of God. So it is with a redeemed soul. The day we apply the blood of Christ by faith to our hearts and are delivered from Satan's bondage dates our new birth. Our spiritual life begins then, and all the years we have lived before that time are not counted in that respect.

6. The "mixed multitude" with the Israelites (v. 38) may have been Egyptians and people from other countries sojourning in Egypt, or possibly the descendants of Egyptians and Hebrews who had intermarried. Whatever the case, they were of mixed principles, partly on the Lord's side and partly on the Egyptians' side. Further on (in Num. 11:4-6) we see them causing trouble and making even the true Israelites discontented. In every great company of God's people we find some of the mixed multitude—those who would have salvation but still hold on to the vanities of the world. They are a dangerous crowd; they will always cause trouble and get those around them discontented with the "narrow way." The church must be careful of these.

7. There is nothing inconsistent with the fact that God rained down severe judgment on some while at the same time He was protecting and blessing others. The Egyptians were experiencing horror while the Israelites were safely fellowshiping in their homes. God's holiness and love always coexist.

8. Notice that the children of Israel not only believed God but obeyed His directions (vv. 28, 35, 50). It was the faith that led to works that brought them salvation.

9. Before leaving this extremely important subject of the Passover, let us observe in order the points in which the Passover typifies redemption. Be sure to look up all references given here.

III. SUMMARY

The Passover chapter must surely be looked upon as a key chapter of the Bible.

Passover	Redemption
1. The sacrifice must be a lamb (v. 3).	1. Christ was the Lamb of God (1 Cor. 5:7).
2. The lamb must be without spot or blemish (v. 5).	2. Christ was without spot or blemish (1 Pet. 1:18-19).
3. It must be in the prime of existence when offered (v. 5).	3. Christ was in the prime of His manhood when offered (33 years old).
4. Lamb's blood is shed that they might have life (vv. 6-7).	4. Christ's blood was shed that all might have life (John 3:16, 1 Pet. 2:24).
5. It is not sufficient that blood is shed, but each one wishing benefit from it must apply it to his door with a bunch of hyssop (vv. 7, 22).	5. It is not sufficient that His blood was shed, but each one wishing benefit from it must apply the blood to his own heart by faith (Rom. 3:25-26; 10:9-10).
6. Blood must be seen from the outside (v. 7).	6. Christ must be openly and publicly confessed before men (Matt. 10:32-33).
7. No safety except behind the blood-stained doors (v. 22).	7. There is no safety except behind the blood of Christ (Mark 16:16).
8. When safe behind the blood, they must feed upon the lamb whose blood had saved them from death (v. 8).	8. When safe behind the blood, we must feed upon Christ, whose blood has saved us from death (John 6:53, 56).
9. The flesh must be eaten with bitter herbs (v. 8).	9. We should constantly remember, in a spirit of contrition, what this redemption cost Christ.
10. The meal must be separated from all leaven (type of sin) (v. 8).	10. We must not practice sin, avoiding even the appearance of evil (1 John 3:9-10).
11. Israelites must maintain the pilgrim attitude: loins girded, shoes on feet, staff in hand (v. 11).	11. Those saved by the blood of Christ should maintain the pilgrim attitude in this world (1 Pet. 2:11; Heb. 11:13).

1. It records the bitter climax of plagues, revealing the judgments of God, and the glorious end of bondage, revealing the grace of God.

2. It relates the auspicious commencement of Israel's sacred era, spotlighting divine election, as well as picturing the supreme type of man's redemption, spotlighting universal invitation.

3. It follows the demise of Pharaoh, type of Satan, and the rise of Moses, type of Christ.

4. It manifests two basic eternal principles: death for sin, and life through the blood.

"This is that night of the Lord to be observed . . ." (12:42).

Lesson 7

The Red Sea

The first eighteen chapters of Exodus relate Israel's deliverance, whereas the remaining chapters concern their worship (see survey chart on p. 9). The deliverance was not in one isolated event. It involved preservation through bondage; provision of a leader; promotion of a spirit of hope of deliverance through promises; protection in the midst of severe plagues; power over the obstacle of the Red Sea; and provision in a strange and hostile wilderness. Such were the varied experiences of Israel over those many years. The lesson of our present study is engaged about Israel's deliverance through the Red Sea from the pursuit of the chariots of Pharaoh.

I. ANALYSIS

Proceed to read the chapters, keeping in mind that although Pharaoh had given the Israelites release from Egypt (12:31), he was not a man of his word; hence it is not surprising to see that he made one last lunge at Israel to try to subdue them. Refer to the map on page 63 for some help on the geography of this narrative.

As you read, follow the procedures and methods of study already suggested in this study guide. Be sure to keep a pencil or pen in hand while reading the Bible text, underlining key words and phrases and making other pertinent notations as you observe them. (As one has said, "The pencil is one of the best eyes.")

The Bible text of this lesson covers almost three chapters, but we will still follow the same procedure of drawing a rectangle chart to record our paragraph study. Make paragraph divisions according to the following chart. (Note: For purposes of simplicity, the number of paragraphs for this section has been reduced to a minimum; you may choose to divide the text into a larger number of paragraphs, e.g., 13:1-10, 11-16.)

13:1	FIRSTBORN
17	ETHAM
22	
14:1	ENTANGLED
10	ISRAEL CRIED
15	WALL
31	
15:1	SONG
21	

1. After recording key words and phrases for each paragraph within the rectangle, determine the main theme of each paragraph. Then look for groupings of paragraphs and record them. Notice the suggestion of groupings shown in the above chart. Try to justify those divisions.

2. What is the atmosphere of the paragraph 13:1-16?

Of 15:1-21?

3. Study the phrase "it is mine" (13:2). Relate this to the present context and to the chapters preceding this study (e.g., compare 12:11*b*, 13). Also relate this spiritually to Romans 12:1.

4. What was the spiritual purpose of the ordinance of unleavened bread for Israel?

Of the ordinance of the firstborn?

5. Notice the progression of atmosphere in the three paragraphs 13:1-22; 14:1-9; 14:10-14. How do Moses' words of 14:13-14 fit into the narrative?

Have you observed any progress in Moses' faith, since his original call (chap. 3)?

6. The statement in 14:2*a* should read, "Speak unto the children of Israel, that they *turn back* and encamp . . . ." Why do you suppose God allowed the Israelites to alter their direction, as though they were "entangled"?

(Note: The exact locations of some of the places of this narrative are unknown to us now. However, you can follow the pattern of the journey by observing the general statements, such as "edge of the wilderness" (13:20), "turn back," and "over against" (14:2). Beyond this, the suggested locations of places on the map on page 63 will still be of help to visualize Israel's movements.)

7. What words assured the Israelites they would see Pharaoh no more?

8. Compare the Israelites' complaint of 14:12, "Let us alone, that we may serve the Egyptians," with the oft-repeated words of God to Pharaoh (e.g., 7:16).

_____

_____

_____

9. Visualize the dramatic action of 14:15-31. Observe how many miracles were wrought in the total sequence of events. Note also the three key words of 14:31: "saw," "feared," and "believed in" (ASV).

10. Why do you suppose so much space is devoted to the songs of Moses, Israel, and Miriam?

_____

_____

Does Moses' praise refer only to past deliverance?

_____

_____

What are the spiritual lessons of 15:1-21?

_____

_____

_____

II. COMMENTS

A. God's Ownership of Israel Declared (13:1-16)

The firstborn of the Hebrews had been saved from the physical death that had overtaken the firstborn of the Egyptians, and now, as though God sought to impress upon them from the very first that they no longer belonged to Pharaoh but to God—that they were not their own but were bought with a price—He commanded Moses to set them aside and sanctify them for the Lord (13:1-2, 11-16). The first thing a soul should realize when saved from spiritual death is that he belongs henceforth to the Lord (1 Cor. 6:19-20).

B. The Roundabout Way to Canaan (13:17-18)

Read 13:17-18 and observe the wisdom of God in not leading the Israelites directly to Canaan. There were at least two reasons for this. One is stated explicitly and the other is implied.

1. Remember the Israelites' condition at this time—a race of liberated slaves, unacquainted with war, government, themselves, and God. If this great multitude of men, women, and children, with their flocks and herds and household goods, had gone directly to Canaan and encountered the enemy entrenched in strong walled cities, versed in all the arts of war and prepared to fight to the death for every inch of territory, they would have become discouraged and returned to Egypt. Of course, God could have worked miracles as He had already done, and, subduing their enemies before them, could have brought them into the land at once; but His plan for them was partly based on a reasonable strategy to avoid the formidable fortresses of Philistia at this time. God's plan was to test the Israelites, but that testing was to confront them *as they were*, and they were not soldiers at this time. (Note: This is not to say that Israel did not have to engage any enemy in battle even in the wilderness way: cf. battle against Amalek, 17:8-13.)

2. God had much to teach the Israelites before He would have them enter the land to stand before the nations of the world as His peculiar treasure, a model for other nations. Remember, Israel was destined for a high calling. The oracles of God were to be committed to this nation. Israel was to be the repository of God's truth, the channel through which, at length, His blessing would flow out to the whole world. And if they were to fill this high position correctly, they had to take time to have God's will fully revealed to them. They were to sit long at God's feet, listen to His instructions, be sure they understood His plan, and learn thoroughly the work He had for them to do and His method for accomplishing that work. Above all, they had to learn how He wanted them to conduct themselves in every particular, both toward God and toward man, and they had to be willing to obey His commands. God wanted *time* with the Israelites, and the long wilderness journey afforded this.

Now, see the application. Even after we are saved, before we can expect to stand before the world as representatives of Christ, we must take time to sit at His feet and learn of Him. We must know His plan, the work He would have accomplished, His methods, and, above all, we must be absolutely willing to surrender our wills to Him.

This is why Bible study is so important for the Christian from the moment of his new birth. The one who has been saved from death should immediately begin to study how to live. Spend much time studying God's Word.

C. Start of the Journey and God's Strange Command (13:19–14:4)

The start of Israel's journey from Egypt gave all promise of success. Pharaoh was not in pursuit (nor was there any reason as yet to expect this); the people had completed one leg of the journey (from Succoth to Etham); and, best of all, they had been sent a constant reminder of God's presence in the form of a miraculous pillar to lead them—a cloud by day and fire by night. But Etham was at the edge of the wilderness (13:20), and now the obstacles were about to appear. God's plan was to bring on a situation involving Pharaoh, to make a final disposition of him and his armies "that the Egyptians may know that I am the Lord" (14:4). Hence His command to have the Israelites "turn back" (the correct rendering of the Hebrew word in 14:2) from Etham and encamp elsewhere (before Pi-hahiroth, over against Baal-zephon), so as to make Pharaoh think they had come up against a "stone wall," were entangled in the land, and thus vulnerable to attack. Such was God's strategy of the turning back. (Note: Baal-zephon is located north of Etham. Such a location accords with the view that the sea that the Israelites crossed [and therefore the sea by which they encamped; 14:2] was not the present Gulf of Suez, but the Reed Sea, the area of marshes and lakes between the gulf and the Mediterranean Sea, now the location of the Suez Canal. The miraculous aspects of the crossing are retained in this geographical identification.

D. Pharaoh's Pursuit and Israel's Fear (14:5-14)

After the first shock of the midnight slaughter had subsided, Pharaoh no doubt began to repent his action of releasing the Israelites. It was a great loss to the monarch to be deprived of 2 million slaves, to say nothing of the jewels and gold and silver with which the Egyptian people had laden them. Work on his great buildings had to cease because he had no workmen. Financially, Pharaoh was ruined. But about this time he heard of the peculiar turnabout that the Hebrews made on their journey. Their capture seemed possible to him, because he did not take into consideration the ways of the Hebrews' God. So, hastily summoning his horses, chariots, and soldiers, he pursued and overtook them, encamping by the sea. The Israelites saw the Egyptians coming, and cried out to God and against Moses. They saw nothing but a fate worse than death before them and believed it would have been better not to have started from Egypt. But Moses' faith won out. He bade them "stand still and see the salvation of the Lord" and assured them that the Lord would fight for them. And what a salvation it was.

The Israelites "cried out unto the Lord" (14:10), but they did not rest in the Lord. Although it did not appear so to them, they were really in no peril whatever because they were in the very place to which God had ordered them, and the Lord Himself was there to defend them. It was only their lack of faith that threw them into such a panic.

Sometimes, when a soul has started a new life with God and looks back, he is filled with fear and discouragement. He seems to see Satan and all his hosts in pursuit. He recognizes some of his old taskmasters (sinful habits or appetites) and remembers the power they had over him. He fears they will overtake him. He feels it is no use trying to live free from them. He almost regrets having started the Christian life. The word to such a defeated Christian is the word Moses gave Israel: "Fear ye not, stand still, and see the salvation of the Lord. . . . *The Lord shall fight for you*" (14:13-14). 1 Corinthians 10:13 is a wonderful promise for times of testing.

E. The Great Deliverance (14:15-31)

At the command of God, as the Israelites in obedience to God began to move forward, Moses stretched his rod out over the sea, and as he did so a strong wind from the east parted the waters, leaving a path through the bed of the sea by which they crossed on *dry* land. The cloud, which had previously gone before them, now removed and stood behind, to cut off their movements from the enemies. In the morning the Egyptians saw what had occurred and boldly and presumptuously plunged in, not awed by the miracle of the parted waters. But God's people were safe on the other side, and at His command Moses again stretched his hand over the sea, and the walls of water rushed together, drowning all the Egyptians in the sea.

This was a marvelous deliverance. Pharaoh's power was broken forever. Never again would the Israelites need to fear what he could do to them. As they realized this, the people burst into songs of thanksgiving and praise (15:1-21). This is the first substantial song of praise heard from the children of Israel, and tragically it is about the last. From this point on, they were murmuring and grumbling all the way on their journey. Nothing pleased

61

them. At every step they found something that did not suit them; they were constantly longing for the things left behind, and made little progress. What was the cause of this sudden change? Exodus 15 starts with a burst of praise, but before its close (vv. 22-27) the murmuring begins and does not cease until the Israelites get nearly to the Promised Land. The explanation? It was one thing to stand on the banks of the sea, finally delivered from their enemies; it was quite another thing to plod on day after day through the wilderness, bearing the burdens and discomforts and trials of the way. The children of Israel lost sight of the goal ahead of them (Canaan); they forgot that God was constantly with them to supply every need; they got their eyes fixed on the discomfort of the way, and murmured against God and against Moses.

F. The Model Song

Read carefully the song that Moses and the children of Israel sang (15:1-21), and notice the contrast it presents to much music today. This song is just one long note of praise to God. There is not a note of self in it from beginning to end. It is all of Him, what He is, what He has done, and what He will do.

It is well for the newborn soul to meditate and sing much of Him.

III. SUMMARY

This account of Exodus might be summarized in four words:

	1. SANCTIFICATION:	"There shall be *no leavened bread* be seen with thee."
13:1-16		
	2. PRESENTATION:	"*I sacrifice* every firstling of my beasts."
		"Of my children *I redeem.*"
13:17– 14:31	3. OBSERVATION:	"Stand still, and *see.*"
15:1-21	4. GLORIFICATION:	"I will *sing* unto the Lord."

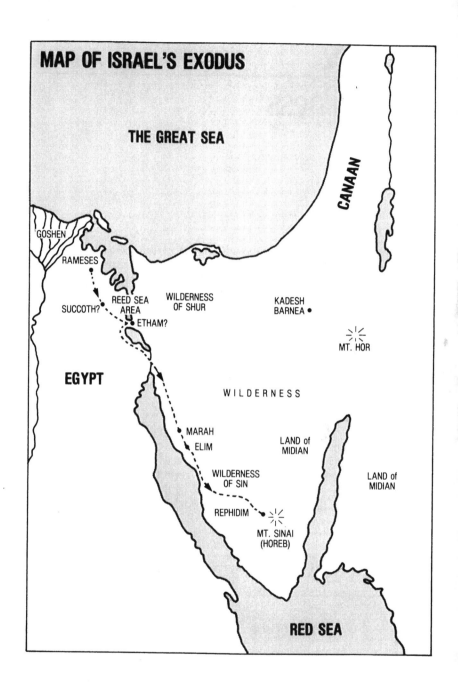

MAP OF ISRAEL'S EXODUS

THE GREAT SEA

CANAAN

GOSHEN

RAMESES

SUCCOTH?

REED SEA AREA

ETHAM?

WILDERNESS OF SHUR

KADESH BARNEA

MT. HOR

EGYPT

WILDERNESS

MARAH

ELIM

LAND of MIDIAN

LAND of MIDIAN

WILDERNESS OF SIN

REPHIDIM

MT. SINAI (HOREB)

RED SEA

Lesson 8

Wilderness

God showed his graciousness and power in delivering Israel completely from the throes of an oppressing enemy, letting the Red Sea close behind the Israelites and thereby ending that era of bondage. Now God continues to show Himself totally sufficient for the trials of a wilderness journey, if His people will only believe and obey.

I. ANALYSIS

The chapters of this lesson might be divided into two main parts, as shown by the charts on page 65, with paragraph divisions indicated. After reading through the passage in one sitting, follow the regular study procedures of this guide, recording your observations on the charts.

1. Notice how the Israelites are the main actors of the first segment (15:22–17:16), whereas segment 18:1-27 centers on Jethro. Compare the atmosphere of 15:22–17:7 with that of 18:1-12. Record this.

2. Notice in the first segment Moses' burdens along the journey.

In what way is 18:1-27 related to the subject of Moses' burdens?

What lessons for the Christian church are taught here?

ISRAEL 15:22—17:16 ISRAEL'S TESTINGS	JETHRO 18:1-27 MOSES' ASSISTANTS
15:22	18:1
27	
16:1	
	13
4	17
9	
22	24
	27
31	
36	
17:1	
8	
14	

3. Record the four major problems of the first segment.

_____

_____

What does each paragraph of chapter 16 contribute to the problem of no food?

_____

_____

_____

4. Concerning Amalek: The Amalekites were descended from Esau (Gen. 36:12). What lesson do you learn from this?

_____

_____

5. In what sense could the attack by the Amalekites be considered a divine punishment for Israel's murmuring?

_____

_____

Notice this is the only enemy opposition that Israel encountered on their journey to Sinai.
6. Note Moses' physical stance while Joshua fought. What does this posture remind you of?

_____

_____

7. What do you learn about Jethro from this account?

_____

_____

What kind of a spiritual experience is indicated by 18:11?

_____

_____

8. What do you learn about Moses from this account?

II. COMMENTS

A. The New Life

The first stage of Israel's journey, considered geographically, was over. Their experiences in Egypt were past. They were now in the second stage of their journey, the wilderness.

No sooner had the children of Israel crossed the narrow strip of water of the Red (or Reed) Sea, than they were standing on a new continent, beginning a new life, with God—not Pharaoh—as

King. The Red Sea rolled between the two territories, effectually dividing them. Just so the human soul has but to turn his back upon Satan, step over the narrow decision line, and he finds himself in a new world, beginning a new life, in which God and not Satan is king.

B. Israel at Marah (15:22-26)

God was taking His people to Sinai, but they had to make four important stops on the way, and at each God taught memorable lessons for them and for us. The first stop was at Marah. (See map.)

Here, after three days' weary march (15:22) without finding water, they had the great disappointment of finding the waters bitter. It is little wonder that they murmured when we consider that they looked upon the circumstances and not to God. Christians should learn a solemn lesson from this. When we first realize that Satan's power over us is broken forever, that we are born of the Spirit, and that, as God's children, we are to live on through the ages with Him, and share in all the delights and beauties and riches with Christ Jesus, our hearts are filled with praise and thanksgiving. But as the days go by, and we march on in life's journey, meeting the trials and disappointments and difficulties which come to every one of us, we lose sight of the glorious goal before us and forget that Christ is with us to supply every need. We get our eyes fixed on the discomforts of the way and only too often grow discouraged and murmur. Our hallelujahs are turned into rebellious murmurings. But how much better to go joyfully forward, our hearts set on the prize of the upward calling, attracting others to the Christian life by our glad behavior.

Murmuring, discontent, wandering, and backsliding are characteristics of that sort of Christian life of which the wilderness is a type. The Spirit-filled Christian life of joy, peace, contentment, and victory, is represented by the possession of Canaan under Joshua, which is a type of this richer, fuller, deeper experience.

Note the miracle which God performed for Moses and the people. God showed Moses a tree, which he cast into the water, causing its bitterness to disappear. Often there comes to us, soon after we become Christians, a disappointment that is extremely bitter and hard to endure. Just at this point, Satan would get our eyes on circumstances and off God, and thus get us discouraged. But we should remember that however bitter the experience, if we put the *Branch*, Christ Jesus, into it, the bitterness will disappear. There is no experience in life so bitter that Christ cannot sweeten it.

C. Israel at Elim (15:27)

"And they came to Elim, where were twelve wells of water and threescore and ten palm trees; and they encamped there by the waters" (15:27).

The people must have been ashamed after their murmuring at Marah to see how abundantly the Lord was able to supply their need. Here were twelve wells, a well for each of the twelve tribes, and the seventy palm trees growing so luxuriantly and speaking to them of the blessing and growth and fruitfulness that comes by abiding. No wonder they settled down and encamped there for a while. Perhaps they learned something of the truth expressed in Psalms 1:3 and 92:12 regarding the righteous man.

D. Israel at the Wilderness of Sin (16:1-36)

The camp moved on to the Wilderness of Sin (the word Sin here has no moral connotation), where another difficulty was encountered. There was nothing to eat. Again their faith failed, and they murmured and regretted that they ever started from Egypt. Such blindness and ingratitude! Because of present discomforts they failed utterly to appreciate the immeasurable advantage of being under God's rule instead of Pharaoh's. Someone had commented on this thus: "The Israelites were much more disposed to complain at the privations met in the path in which God led them than at the hardships endured in Pharaoh's service; just as many today complain more at the privations of God's service than of the hardships of Satan's bondage. When people wish themselves back in Egypt (a life of worldliness and sin), they forget both the bitterness of the old life and the blessings of the new."

Notice the love and patience of God in meeting this grumbling with a gracious promise (16:4). But God proved how much better He was than their old master. Instead of making them work without pay, He rained down food already prepared for them each morning. All through the forty years of wandering the manna did not once fail them.

In our journey of life as Christians, the Bread prepared for our souls is Christ (see John 6:48-51, 63). Are you gathering it fresh every morning? Many Christians will not go to the Bible each day for spiritual food, and then they wonder what they are so weak—why they stumble and fall into sin so easily and accomplish so little for God. Just as we could not expect to grow strong physically without food for the body, so we cannot expect to grow strong spiritually without food for the soul. Once a lady complained to me about her spiritual weakness and asked what was the trouble. I said, "Do you read your Bible every day?" In the greatest surprise she answered, "No. What has that to do with it? I read it on Sunday, and during the week if I have time I read it a little." If this lady had complained of her physical weakness, and I had asked, "Do you eat every day?" she would hardly have replied, "No, what has that to do with the matter? I eat on Sunday, and during the week if I have time I take a bite or two." If she had, we should all agree as to the absurdity of her reasoning; yet many argue like that when it comes to regular daily Bible study.

God's purpose in giving the manna each day, and just enough for the day, was to test whether the people would obey. Some of them failed the very first test (vv. 19-20).

E. God's Provision for Rest (16:22-30)

God supplied not only food but also rest for the Israelites (16:23). Notice that God did not harshly command the keeping of the Sabbath but graciously gave one day in seven on which to rest. Some did not appreciate the gift (16:27-30), and later on at Sinai, God, for their own good, commanded the Israelites to observe the Sabbath.

F. Israel at Rephidim (17:1–18:27)

At length the Israelites reached Rephidim (17:1), and found no water. They were meeting difficulties at every step, but each new difficulty was only another opportunity to see more of God's goodness and power, and when seen in that light the difficulties should have been welcomed. Had their faith been like Abraham's, they would have said, "Now we shall see some fresh manifestation of our God." How few of us meet trials and difficulties in this spirit! Too often, like the Israelites, we meet trials with murmurings instead of faith.

Notice how slow the Israelites were to learn; one would naturally think, after having seen God's power over water at the Red Sea and at Marah, and His abundant supply at Elim, that the Israelites would have learned to trust Him for water here. But they seemed incapable of faith. Notice that there was no word of reproof from God but only patient, loving supplying of their needs (17:4-6). At the command of God, Moses smote the rock, and streams of refreshing water began to flow forth before that thirsty throng. In 1 Corinthians 10:4 we are told that this rock is a type of Christ. When Christ was smitten on the cross, streams of blessing flowed.

Three important events occurred at Rephidim. The first was the smitten rock. The second was the fight with Amalek, where Joshua led the men out to battle (17:8-10). Could it not be that God allowed this enemy attack as judgment for the people's murmurings? Read 17:11, and notice that while Moses' hands were upheld in intercession, Israel gained the victory; and so as usual their help came from above. When in bondage in Egypt they could have looked in every direction and not a nation on earth would have helped them. But when they looked up and cried to God He sent them deliverance. At the Red Sea, Marah, Elim, and Rephidim it was ever the same. God was evidently trying to teach them the lesson that He would have all His children learn—in this new life with Him they were to depend absolutely and implicitly upon Him for everything.

When there comes a bitter experience, go to God for comfort. Sweet as human sympathy may be, it is only God who can effectually wipe away tears and heal broken hearts. When the soul is faint and hungry, seek not to satisfy with anything this world can afford; feed upon the true Bread from heaven. When athirst, drink of the Living Water.

The third event that occurred at Rephidim was the conversion of Jethro and the appointing of the rulers to help Moses in the tremendous task of counseling (chap. 18). The children of Israel was now near the home of Moses' father-in-law, and Jethro brought to Moses his wife and two children (18:1-6).

The story of Jethro's conversion is a beautiful one indeed. Jethro came to Moses rejoicing over all he had heard about God's gracious and powerful ways and confessing his faith in God, saying, "Now I know that the Lord is greater than all gods." He offered a burnt offering and sacrifices unto God, fellowshiped with Moses, Aaron, and the elders, and offered helpful advice to Moses.

Jethro was concerned over Moses' exhausting schedule. He believed Moses should continue to intercede for his people over the weightier matters and teach them the statutes of the Lord, but he should delegate to able rulers the authority to judge the innumerable smaller matters. Moses took Jethro's advice, and Jethro "went his way into his own land," a very content, new man!

III. SUMMARY

The account of these chapters reveals these two parallel lines of truth concerning God and Moses:

1. In the situation of an ungrateful people's MURMURING, there is hope in the LONGSUFFERING of GOD, with the solution in HIS ABSOLUTE SUFFICIENCY (15:22–17:16).

2. In the situation of the DAILY NEEDS of 2 million people, there is hope if the UNTIRING SERVANT Moses can endure; the solution is found in DISPENSABLE MOSES sharing his load (18:1-27).

In summary, when compared with the previous section, the chapters of this lesson present a vivid contrast.

15:1-21	15:22—17:14	18:1-27
THE PEOPLE'S PRAISE TO GOD	THE PEOPLE'S MURMURING	AN OUTSIDER'S PRAISE AND HELP

Lesson 9

The Law

This is an entirely new section in the book of Exodus, for the events of these chapters marked a new era in Israel's history. Refer back to the survey chart (p. 9), and review the previous sections as introduction to these next lessons. Geographically, the progress is:

Israel in Egypt—Israel in Sinai—Israel at Sinai

Study the other identifications made concerning the general content of these sections. Chapters 19-40 mainly concern Israel's worship of God. Review the four sections of these chapters as shown on the survey chart: the giving of the law (chaps. 19-24); the Tabernacle instructions (chaps. 25-31); the idolatry of the people (chaps. 32-34); and the construction of the Tabernacle (chaps. 35-40). To worship is to acknowledge a higher authority, and there is no authority where there is no law. So God began to spell out the explicit form of worship He wanted by giving them laws as their "schoolmaster." The importance of the law to Israel is seen by the space devoted to it in the Pentateuch—about half of Exodus, most of Leviticus, the first part of Numbers, and much of Deuteronomy.

I. ANALYSIS

This section contains the well-known Ten Commandments, and one might say from an overall view that 20:1-21 is the key passage of the section. The purpose of this study is not only to learn what is taught by the Ten Commandments but also to see the context in which they are recorded in Exodus. Observe from your study that the surrounding context of the Ten Commandments is colorful, rich, and edifying. Learn the context of the commandments, and you will appreciate them more than ever before.

To catch the spirit and atmosphere of these chapters (19-24), first read them through in one sitting. Then on a sheet of paper

72

held horizontally, block out the following five rectangles, each representing a segment of the passage. (Note: Some paragraphs have been intentionally combined here.)

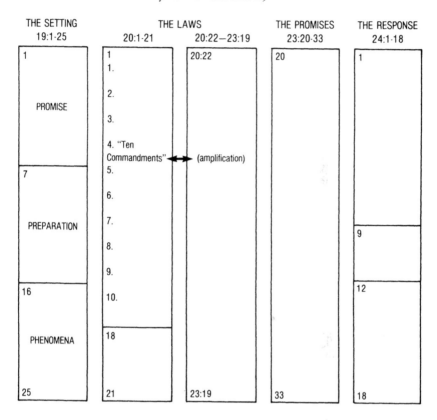

THE SETTING 19:1-25
THE LAWS 20:1-21
20:22—23:19
THE PROMISES 23:20-33
THE RESPONSE 24:1-18

Notice from the charts shown that help has been given you in identifying the content of the segments. First, confirm in your own mind the appropriateness of the suggestions; make any changes you wish to. Then answer the following questions, recording your observations on your own charts.

1. How is the promise of 19:1-6 different from the promises of 23:20-33?

_____

_____

2. Compare the atmosphere of chapter 19 with that of chapter 24.

_____

3. Note the references in chapter 19 (implied or explicit) to *spiritual* life. What is meant by the phrase "ye shall be a peculiar treasure unto me" (19:5)?

_____

Compare Titus 2:14 and 1 Peter 2:9.

_____

Record the numerous audible or visual phenomena. People's reaction?

_____

How were the events of chapter 19, a fitting setting for God's giving the law?

_____

4. Read 20:1-21. Does the phrase "ten commandments" appear in this text? Now read Exodus 34:28 and Deuteronomy 4:13. Were the commandments intended as a way of salvation, or as a guide of living for people already redeemed?

_____

Are any promises of blessing found?

_____

Which commandments show our duty to God?

_____

Which show our duty to man?

_____

What of God's character is revealed by these laws?

_____

_____

_____

What is revealed of man's character?

_____

_____

Do the Ten Commandments apply to today, and if so, how?

_____

_____

_____

5. Are the laws given in 20:22–23:19 different from the Ten Commandments, or are they laws growing out of the great principles?

_____

_____

6. Read 24:1-8. Relate the three words "covenant," "obedient," and "blood." How important is obedience in Christian living?

_____

_____

What should be the basic motivation for obedience?

_____

7. Exodus 24:11 says "also they saw God." In what sense can a man see God?

_____

Compare it with 33:20. What was God's basic purpose in manifesting Himself in audible and visible situations?

_____

_____

8. List ten spiritual lessons that you have learned from these chapters.

_____

_____

_____

_____

_____

_____

II. COMMENTS

A. Arrival at Mount Sinai (19:1-2)

Just three months after starting from Egypt, the people arrived at Sinai (19:1-2). This great lone mountain was to be their school-house for the next year. All through the remainder of Exodus, Leviticus, and a part of Numbers, the setting of the action is here. God had already taught them much of Himself. His power and wisdom were revealed in Egypt, and during the three months along the way He had taught them of His love and mercy and watch-care over them. But now they were to enter into deeper lessons.

This territory was not new to Moses. Moses had lived nearby with his father-in-law for forty years (see Acts 7:30, 38; Ex. 18:5), and it was here that God first met him and gave him his commission to go and deliver the people (3:1-12). Notice how Moses seemed eager to seek another interview with God on the same holy ground (19:3), and how God instantly responded and "called unto him." When we draw nigh unto God He is always ready to draw nigh unto us (James 4:8). Moses was frequently found separated from man and in seclusion with God (Ex. 20:21; 24:15-18; 34:2, 4; Deut. 5:5, 30-31; 9:12, 18-19).

B. God's Reminder and Proposal (19:3-6)

Read carefully 19:3-6, and notice the following four things:

1. Jehovah reminded His people (v. 4) that hitherto they had been the objects of His free grace. (Grace means unmerited favor.) They had done nothing to earn their deliverance from Egypt; indeed they had been untrue to God before He delivered them and had complained of God's dealings afterward. But God in His

76

great love and pity for them, and in fulfillment of His promise to His friend Abraham had taken them from Egypt unto Himself. (God compares Himself, in a beautiful figure of speech, to the eagle bearing his young upon his wings.) Now that the Israelites were free and brought nigh unto Him, God had a dazzling proposal to make to them. He wanted to enter into a covenant with them. He made them a conditional promise. He said if they would do a certain thing (viz., obey His voice and keep His covenant, v. 5), He would do wonderful things for them. On the one condition of *obedience* Israel was to be Jehovah's "peculiar treasure." They were to be a "kingdom of priests," that is, persons with the right of access to God and standing as mediators between God and other men. They were to be a "holy nation."

2. All these things that were promised to Israel under the dispensation of law on the condition of obedience are freely given to every believer under the present dispensation of grace, unconditionally (1 Peter 2:9-10; Rev. 1-6), but not without heavy responsibility (e.g., 1 Peter 2:9*b*).

3. God did not give the law to *save Israel*. He gave the law so that they might know how to live for Him and thus be unto Him the "peculiar treasure."

We are not saved by works; we are saved by faith in the blood of Christ. After we are saved we may gain rich reward and attain unto a high Christian character by faithfully performing God's will.

4. How little Israel understood their own frailty and proneness to sin when they so readily and almost flippantly consented to the condition of obedience (v. 8). Within a few weeks they had broken every one of God's laws, proving that "the heart is deceitful above all things, and desperately wicked" (Jer. 17:9).

C. God Appears and Speaks (19:7-25)

This intimate conversation of God with Moses at this time is awe-inspiring. Years afterward, when Moses was making his farewell address just before his death, he referred to this scene and asked if from the beginning of time such a great thing had been known. "For ask now of the days that are past, which were before thee, since the day that God created man upon the earth, and ask from the one side of heaven unto the other, whether there hath been any such thing as this great thing is, or hath been heard like it? Did ever people hear the voice of God speaking out of the midst of the fire, as thou hast heard, and live? Out of heaven he made thee to hear his voice, that he might instruct thee: and upon earth he shewed thee his great fire; and thou heardest his words out of the midst of the fire" (Deut. 4:32-33, 36).

Try to picture the scene that morning when the Lord came down and talked to Israel. First the roar of thunder struck and the lightning began playing around the mountains; then the voice of the trumpet sounded so exceedingly loud that all the people trembled, and even Moses, holy man that he was, said, "I exceedingly fear and quake" (Heb. 12:21). The mountain was smoking and rocking and quaking and still the trumpet sounded louder and louder, and the terror of the people increased. Then God spoke with an audible voice and gave the law. Israel must have been impressed with the infinite majesty and holiness and power of God—have we today lost that sense? Notice how the people were warned against any unhallowed curiosity (19:12-13, 21-22). This should be a warning not to talk flippantly of God, question His doings, or peer lightly into the things that concern Him alone. The further lesson which the Christian must learn from the awesome phenomena of Mount Sinai is the contrasting truth of blessed intimate access to the throne of this very God. Read Hebrews 12:18-24 for the wonderful applications.

D. Ten Commandments (20:1-21)

It is of the utmost importance to understand the true character and object of the law as set forth in the Ten Commandments. Many people consider the keeping of the law as the means of salvation. Often when urged to become a Christian, some will answer, "I am doing as well as I can," the idea seeming to be that God saves as a reward for well-doing.

But no one can ever be saved by *doing*, that is, apart from believing. The doing is the fruit of believing. (Read Gal. 2:16; James 2:26; Acts 16:29-31.) It is useless to think of being saved by the law, because God has told us in James 2:10, "Whosoever shall keep the whole law, and yet offend in one point, he is guilty of all." If we do not keep it absolutely in every point throughout all our lifetime from birth to death (and no one but the Lord Jesus Christ ever did), we cannot be saved by the law, any more than one suspended by a chain over a deep abyss could be saved by the chain if he should break only *one* link. This one broken link would be fatal to him. So it is with the law.

Then what is the purpose of the law? It shows God's standard of perfection and what a person would have to measure up to if saved by his own works. The Ten Commandments set forth what man ought to be, and by contrast what he really is, convincing him of his need for cleansing by a holy God. Galatians 3:24 states the place which the law occupies in the scheme of redemption: "The law was our schoolmaster to bring us unto Christ." It brings us to Christ in the sense that it shows us what sin is in God's sight and points us to the Lamb slain for our sins.

Notice a few things about Exodus 20. The commandments are addressed in the singular number. "Thou shalt have no other gods before me." Not "ye," as though speaking to the whole congregation in general, but "thou," addressing each individual.

Notice the two great divisions of the law, Godward and manward. The first four commandments tell us our duty toward God, the last six our duty toward our fellowman. Christ summed up the whole law in Matthew 22:37-40, observing these two divisions. Love is surely the fulfilling of the law, for if we loved the Lord with all our heart, soul, and mind, we would not break any of the first four; and if we loved our neighbor as ourselves, we would break none of the last six.

Some people contend that since these commandments were given to Israel, and since we are not under the dispensation of law but are living in the new dispensation of grace, therefore these commands are not binding upon us. It is true that this divine law was primarily given to Israel and that it was fulfilled in Christ (Col. 2:14, 16-17; 2 Cor. 3:7-11); but every one of these commandments except the fourth is specifically reiterated in the New Testament as a spiritual standard glorifying God in one's living.

In 20:2 God said: "I . . . have brought thee out of the land of Egypt," and because He had done so much for the Israelites they were to do His will as expressed in the commandments He gave. Christians have no less a motivation for obeying God's Word.

Observe how God reveals His character in the law. His *condescension* is seen in occupying Himself with such details of daily life as the death of an ox, the loan of a garment, or the loss of a tooth (21:28; 22:26; 21:27). His *justice* is seen in the even balance held between the rich and the poor, and in punishment for the guilty versus protection for the innocent. Also man's character is revealed. He is shown to be entirely capable of committing all the dreadful sins here mentioned, or laws against them would never have been made. If there were no flood to be resisted, God would not build a dam.

E. The Law Amplified (20:22–23:19)

In Exodus 20:1-21 God gives the law in outline, and in 20:22–23:19 He gives the law in detail. That is, first God laid down the great eternal principles, and then He gave amplified applications of these principles to ordinary everyday life.

79

There are laws governing the master and servant (21:1-11); injuries to the person (21:12-36); property rights (22:1-15); crimes against humanity (22:16–23:9); the land and the Sabbath (23:10-13); and the three national feasts (23:14-19). These are the laws growing out of the general principles laid down in the Ten Commandments. (Cf. Ex. 20:13; 21:12-15, 18-20.)

F. God's Promises (23:20-23); **and the People's Responses** (24:1-18)

From 23:20-33 observe the many things God promised to do for the Israelites when they reached their promised land. But it was all on the condition of their obedience! (See 23:22.) When Moses read God's Word in the audience of the people, they promised to obey (24:3, 7). Moses even sprinkled the people with blood of the covenant to impress upon them the stand they had taken. How faithful they would be remained to be seen.

In the last part of Exodus 24, Moses was called up to the mountain to be alone with God for forty days, and God revealed to him the pattern for His Tabernacle. Moses left people encamped at the foot of the mountain with Aaron and Hur in charge. This begins the narrative of the next lesson.

III. SUMMARY

Summarize in your own words the narrative of these chapters of Exodus. Use the following outline as your guide:
    A. THE SETTING
    1. Promise
    2. Preparation
    3. Phenomena
    B. THE LAWS
    1. Basic Laws
    2. Laws in detail
    C. THE PROMISES
    D. THE RESPONSE

Lesson 10

Tabernacle Instructions

In the last lesson Moses left the children of Israel encamped at the foot of Mount Sinai with Aaron and Hur in charge, and he himself went up the mountain for forty days to confer with God regarding a house of worship (the Tabernacle) which God wanted constructed. God also gave Moses, in permanent tables of stone, the law that He had delivered orally to Israel.

Chapters 25-31 of Exodus record the specifications and instructions God gave Moses concerning the Tabernacle that the Israelites were to contrast. Chapters 35-40 record Israel's obedience in constructing the Tabernacle as God had directed. The relationship of these two sections to each other is shown here:

EXODUS 19-40

19	25	32	35	40
LAW	TABERNACLE INSTRUCTIONS	IDOLATRY	TABERNACLE CONSTRUCTION	

How the *construction* faithfully followed the *instructions* will be seen in Lesson 12.

Before going any further in this study, acquaint yourself with the names and locations of the items of the Tabernacle as shown by the diagram accompanying the lesson.

I. ANALYSIS

In your first reading of chapters 25-31 do not look for the details of the specifications; rather watch for statements of purpose (e.g.,

81

"that it may be a memorial"; 30:16), and other phrases of explicit spiritual lessons (e.g., "every man that giveth it willingly with his heart"; 25:2). Underline such phrases in your Bible.

Next observe the order in which Exodus presents the Tabernacle specifications. Chapters 25-27 describe both the structure and furniture of the Tabernacle and the court; chapters 28 and 29 describe the ministry of Aaron and the priests in connection with the people's worship; chapter 30 returns to the subject of the Tabernacle pattern; chapter 31 is an appendix, identifying the special workers, reminding of the Sabbath and the workdays, and concluding with a brief but important notice of God giving Moses the two tables of stone. Let the following outline chart help you fix in your mind the organization of these chapters.

EXODUS 25-31
INTRO: 25:1-9

TABERNACLE AND FURNITURE		
CHAPTERS 25-27 Tabernacle furniture 25:10-40 Tabernacle structure chapter 26 Court's brazen altar 27:1-8 Court pattern 27:9-21		CHAPTER 30 **Other items** Altar of incense 30:1-10 Continual fellowship Ransom offering 30:11-16 People's sin Laver 30:17-21 Holy oil 30:22-33 Holy incense 30:34-38 Cleanliness and holiness

	PRIESTLY MINISTRY		APPENDIX
	CHAPTERS 28-29 Priests' garments chapter 28 Priests' consecration 29:1-37 Priests' key offering 29:38-44 Conclusion 29:45-46		CHAPTER 31 CRAFTSMEN (workers) SABBATH (work and rest days) TABLES OF STONE (Word of God)

After you have read these chapters again, read Hebrews 8:1–10:18. Then answer the following questions (answers supplied by both the Exodus and Hebrews passages):

1. Where the the materials for the Tabernacle construction originally come from?

_____

_____

Why did God want a tabernacle built?

_____

_____

2. Was the Tabernacle permanently located?

_____

_____

What is the spiritual lesson here?

_____

_____

3. The "testimony" of 25:16 was the tables of stone containing the Ten Commandments. What significance did this attach to the Ark of the Covenant?

_____

_____

What do you learn from 25:22?

_____

_____

4. Name the pieces of Tabernacle furniture described in chapter 25.

_____

_____

What did each signify to the Israelites?

_____

_____

_____

5. Why is the segment about the priests (chaps. 28-29) inserted in the middle of the description of the furniture of the Tabernacle?

Keep in mind that everything in the Bible is recorded where it is for a reason.

___

6. Why did God have such elaborate garments made for the priest? See 28:2.

___

___

7. Study the five symbolic acts of the priests' consecration of chapter 29, and tell the spiritual significance of each:
a. Washing (v. 4)

___

b. Investiture (vv. 5-9)

___

c. Anointing (v. 7)

___

d. Sacrifice (vv. 10-21)

___

e. Filling the hands (vv. 22-28)

___

8. Compare the frequency of the burnt offering (29:38-39) and the incense offering (30:7).

___

___

What did each offering signify?

___

___

___

9. What was the symbolism behind the ransom offering (30:11-16)?

___

___

10. Notice the repetition of the word "holy" in 30:22-38. What is the lesson?

___

11. In your own way, relate the three paragraphs of chapter 31 to each other (1-11; 12-17; 18). What do the paragraphs contribute to the story of this lesson?

_____

_____

12. List some of the interpretations made by Hebrews 8:1–10:18 of the symbols and types of this lesson.

_____

_____

_____

_____

13. What is the best lesson you have learned in studying the Tabernacle?

_____

_____

_____

II. COMMENTS

A. God's Reason for Wanting the Tabernacle Built

Why did God want a tabernacle built? (See 25:8). God desired to dwell among His people, so He told the Israelites that if they would build Him a tent, or tabernacle, he would come and dwell among them. Not because *He* or the service of worship needed the material building itself, but because the visible Tabernacle and its many objects were to serve as object lessons—through symbol and type—and also as continual reminders to the Israelites of the precious truth of God's dwelling among them. Beyond this, the Tabernacle was one of the grand forerunner truths which God taught His people, anticipating the incarnation of His Son Jesus. In Exodus God came down and dwelt among men in a house made of wood and gold. Fifteen hundred years later He came again and dwelt among men for thirty-three and a half years, this time not in a house made of wood and gold but in a house of flesh and bones, the body of the Lord Jesus Christ. "And the Word became flesh, and tabernacled among us . . . " (John 1:14*a*, ASV margin). Christ was God incarnate, so that God could truly dwell *with us*. The name of God, "Immanuel," literally means, "God *(el)* with us *(immanu)."* This first house, the Tabernacle, which we are studying, is merely a foreshadowing, a type of Christ.

To many the Tabernacle seems to be simply a "Jewish antiquity with no voice or meaning for us." But many of God's children are finding it to be a most wonderful type of Christ. It is a type in many ways, but we are considering it here only in one way, as a type of the Person and work of the Lord Jesus Christ.

B. Structure of Tabernacle

The plan of the Tabernacle, as shown by the following diagram, was basically simple. This was partly because of its portable character, having to be transported by the Israelites on their wilderness journeys. The laver and brazen altar were located in the court, though they were an essential part of the Tabernacle ceremonies.

PLAN OF THE JEWISH TABERNACLE

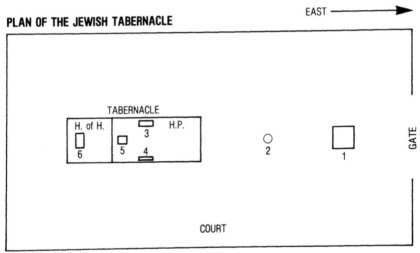

DIMENSIONS (one cubit equals approximately 1½ feet)
COURT—100 BY 50 CUBITS
GATE—20 CUBITS
TABERNACLE—30 BY 10 BY 10 CUBITS
H.P. = HOLY PLACE—20 BY 10 BY 10 CUBITS
H. of H. = HOLY OF HOLIES—10 BY 10 BY 10 CUBITS

FURNITURE
1. BRAZEN ALTAR
2. LAVER
3. TABLE OF SHOWBREAD
4. GOLDEN CANDLESTICK
5. ALTAR OF INCENSE
6. ARK OF THE COVENANT

C. Court (27:9-19)

The Tabernacle was surrounded by a court. This court was made by placing posts in the ground and stretching around them white linen curtains. The posts were connected by silver bands, the redemption money of the children of Israel (see Ex. 27:17; 30:12-16; Num. 3:44-51). There was but one way of entering the court, and that was by the gate (see diagram), which was 20 cubits wide and hung with a veil in which appeared the colors blue, purple, scarlet, and white (linen) (27:16). These colors prevailed throughout the Tabernacle. The court was 100 cubits long and 50 cubits wide (27:18). (A cubit is about 1 1/2 feet.)

D. The Boards and Coverings (26:1-30)

It was necessary for the Israelites to have a building that could be easily taken down and set up, because of their wilderness wanderings. The Tabernacle (other names for the Tabernacle are dwelling, tent of meeting, tent of testimony) was made of forty-eight boards covered with gold and dropped into sockets sunk into the sand. There were twenty of these boards on each side and eight across the back (26:15-30). The building had no floor, but the ceiling was a marvelously wrought covering composed of ten coupled curtains (26:1-6) embroidered with the figures of the cherubim, the heavenly creatures. This was stretched across the top and came almost to the ground on each side of the building. Above this curtain was a covering of white goats' hair (26:7-13); above that was a covering of rams' skins dyed red (26:14); and above that, to protect from weather, was a covering of goatskins, hiding from the outside all inner beauty (26:14). There were four coverings in all.

The Tabernacle was divided into two rooms. The smaller room, which was a complete cube of ten cubits each way, was called the holy of holies; the larger room was called the holy place. These two rooms were divided by a veil (26:31-33). The priests ministered in the holy place daily; into the holy of holies the high priest entered only once a year, alone. (Read Hebrews 6-10.)

E. The Furniture

The Tabernacle contained six pieces of furniture. In the holy of holies there was one piece; in the holy place there were three pieces, and in the court, two pieces. The one in the holy of holies (no. 6 in diagram) was called the Ark of the Covenant. This was a wooden box covered with gold, in which was kept the law written on stone, a pot of the manna, and Aaron's rod that budded and blossomed. The "lid" of the box was the mercy seat, sometimes spoken of as a separate piece of furniture. At each end was the figure of a cherub, and between the figures was the wonderful Shekinah fire, token of the presence of God. So this piece might appropriately be called the throne of God.

Just outside the veil (no. 5) stood the altar of incense, made of wood covered with gold; on the south side of the holy place was the candlestick (no. 4) made of solid gold, having seven lights; on the north side the table of showbread (no. 3) with the twelve loaves that became the food of the priests. Outside the Tabernacle was the laver (no. 2), which was for the cleansing of the priests; and between it and the gate was the brazen altar (no. 1), at which the sinning Israelite brought a substitute to die in his place, atoning for his sin—a clear type of the atoning work of Christ.

F. Symbolism of the Tabernacle

As shown earlier, 1 Corinthians 10:1-11 and Hebrews 8:1–10:18 are two key New Testament passages that serve as a basis for interpreting persons, events, and things of the Old Testament Tabernacle service as *types* of New Testament truths. The Hebrew passage cites only the major items of the Tabernacle, not attempting to be exhaustive concerning the details; it is proper interpretative procedure for the Bible student to look for types or analogies even in the smaller details of each whole item (e.g., the colors), provided a spirit of proper balance is maintained, without straining the interpretation and application. This is the spirit in which the following interpretations are offered.

1. *First, as a whole.* Taken as a whole, the Tabernacle typifies Christ's Person. This tent was, in outward appearance, at least partly similar to those in which the Israelites dwelt. The sun beat down upon the Tabernacle as upon the other smaller tents. The winds swept around it just as they did around the other tents. The Tabernacle passed through al the vicissitudes of weather and travel from Sinai to Canaan as did the other tents. But the difference was that the Tabernacle was God's uniquely designated dwelling place, *the* tent of tents in the center of the Israelite camp.

So it is with the Person of Christ. He had a human body like ours, presenting much the same external appearance. The sun of adversity beat down upon Him just as mercilessly as upon any member of the human family. The winds of temptation swept around Him as they did around others. He passed through the experiences of life, from birth to death, as other men did. But the difference was that in Christ's body God Himself was dwelling. "For in him dwelleth all the fullness of the Godhead bodily" (Col. 2:9).

2. *Second, in detail.* Not only does the Tabernacle, taken as a whole, typify the Person of Christ, but each detail or article of furniture typifies some phase of Christ's work for man. In the New Testament we are told of many phases of Christ's work. In one place He is presented as our Substitute; in another as the one who cleanses the regenerates us. Again, He is shown to be the Bread of Life, the Light of the World, the Good Shepherd, and the Vine.

There is no difficulty in understanding that He is able to be all these different things for us; yet many have never seen that these same phases of His work were foreshadowed in the Tabernacle furniture. In the brazen altar we see Christ our Substitute; in the laver, Christ our Cleanser and Regenerator; in the candlestick, Christ our Light; in the table of showbread, Christ our Bread of Life; in the altar of incense, Christ our Intercessor; and in the mercy seat, Christ our Propitiation.

3. *Third, order of furniture.* Observe the magnificent typical lesson in the very order in which the furniture was arranged. At one extreme, in the holy of holies, was the Ark of the Covenant (no. 6 in diagram)—God's throne. At the other extreme, by the gate, was the brazen altar (no. 1), which typifies the cross of Christ. No man can reach God's throne except by the cross.

We might imagine ourselves standing at the Ark of the Covenant. We are surrounded by golden walls; above is the beautiful curtain with figures of the heavenly creatures; the Ark of gold shows the cherubim bending over the mercy seat; and above the mercy set is manifested God's presence in the Shekinah fire. There is nothing here but light, beauty, love, worship, and God's presence. But what a contrast when we stand at the brazen altar! Here there is nothing but suffering, blood, and death, as the substitutes die in place of the sinners.

Great as is the contrast between these two extremes, it is but a faint picture of the contrast between the two extremes which Christ experienced for us—His Father's throne in glory and the cross of Calvary. First, He was with His Father, surrounded by the worshiping hosts of heaven, where there was only light, beauty, love, worship, and His Father's presence. But He laid aside His glory and stepped down from the throne—down to the cross of Calvary where nothing awaited Him but suffering, blood, and death. And why? So that He might snatch us from the power of Satan and take us back with Him to His home in glory, if only we would believe on Him and let Him lead us into His Father's presence.

In Philippians 2:5-11 this journey that Christ made from the throne to the cross and back again is set forth in a beautiful way. There are seven steps down (vv. 6-8) and seven steps up (vv. 9-11). Someone has beautifully said that all the way from the throne to the cross is marked by the footprints of love, and all the way back from the cross to the throne is sprinkled with the blood of atonement. It was love that brought Christ down, and it is the blood that takes us up.

In the Tabernacle we are taught by objects how to approach God just as we are taught by words in the New Testament. Look at the diagram and observe that if we as guilty sinners, having broken God's law, and consequently having come under condemnation of death, wish to get to God, we must accept Christ as Substitute (Acts 16:31; John 1:29). This is the message of the brazen altar. But Christ can do more for us than save us from the *penalty* of sin. He can cleanse us from the *power* of sin and give us a new life. So the next step is to take Christ as our Cleanser and Regenerator (John 3:5—the laver). Then we must feed upon Christ (John 6:35— table of showbread). Next we must let Him be our Light and Guide (John 8:12—candlestick). And He is the One who intercedes for us and through whom our prayers reach God (John 14:13-14; chap. 17—altar of incense). Notice that all these references are in John. The order of truth there presented exactly corresponds to that presented in the Tabernacle.

The Tabernacle speaks of Christ in other ways. Even its material and colors speak of Him. The wood speaks of His humanity, the gold of His divinity. There is white for purity, blue for promise or prophecy, purple for royalty, and red for blood. There is no black in the Tabernacle as black denotes sin or judgment.

You will find it a spiritually rewarding experience to reread the text of Exodus, which describes the furniture of the Tabernacle, keeping in mind the New Testament antitypes (that which the Old Testament type stands for) mentioned above, and looking for other spiritual truths in the details of the furniture. Also, do not overlook the interpretations and applications of such important items as the continual burnt offerings, the Sabbath day of rest, and the word written "by the finger of God."

III. SUMMARY

The supreme truth of the Tabernacle is the fact that God came down to dwell among men. But this does not automatically bring all men into the family of God. The various other truths written about the Tabernacle complete the story of God's dwelling with His people:

A. ACCESS to a holy God (e.g., by blood of the altar)

B. CONTINUAL FELLOWSHIP (e.g., daily burnt offerings, incense)

C. SERVICE to God —priests
—craftsmen
—days of work, and day of rest

D. SUSTENANCE —Word of God

Lesson 11

Idolatry

A s we heard God on the mount giving directions to Moses, we were occupied with the pattern of the Tabernacle, that marvelous building that foreshadowed the Person and work of Christ. In the Tabernacle we saw revealed something of God's holiness and love and provision for man's needs. It was a beautiful picture of God's heart for man.

But now, as we turn our attention to the people at the foot of the mountain, we see quite a contrast. It is like turning the eyes from the matchless beauty of a summer sky to the mire and filth of a city's back alley.

God was on the mountaintop planning a wonderful tabernacle for the people, planning to come down and dwell among them and give them His constant companionship. But how unworthy of such companionship they appeared. They had reviled God and were dancing around an idol that their own hands had made. It is ever thus. While God plans a wonderful future for mankind, man spurns the future for the revelry of sin today.

The chapters which we have under consideration teach some remarkable and much needed lessons.

I. ANALYSIS

First, read through the three chapters, catching the changes in atmosphere and making your usual observations of key words and phrases. Draw the following segmented rectangles on a sheet of paper, marking the paragraph divisions as shown on the next page.
1. As you reread each paragraph, record key phrases on your analytical chart, following whatever outline help has been given by the chart shown on the next page.

People's Sin 32:1-10 SIN AND JUDGMENT	MOSES'	Moses' Intercession 32:11—33:23 INTERCESSION	God's Restoring Grace 24:1-35 RENEWAL

THE SIN

GOD'S JUDGMENT

1   CALF

7   STIFFNECKED

10

INTERCESSION

RIGHTEOUS WRATH

EXHORTATION

CONTINUED INTERCESSION

AGONY

OBEDIENCE

REWARD

32:11   REMEMBER

15   ANGER

25   3,000

30   FORGIVE

35

33:1   NOT IN MIDST

7   TABERNACLE

12   MY PRESENCE

23

1   2 TABLES

10   COVENANT

29   FACE SHONE

35

2. Contrast the people's attitude to Moses in the first paragraph (32:1-6) with that of the last (34:29-35). What has happened in between?

_____

_____

3. In what sense was the sin so corrupt? (32:1-10).

_____

_____

Was the judgment determined by God a righteous and equitable judgment?

_____

_____

In what large way was Aaron responsible for the people's sin?

_____

_____

What falsehood did Aaron tell Moses?

_____

4. List all the things you learn about Moses from these verses (32:11–33:23).

_____

_____

About God.

_____

_____

How is Moses a type of Christ here?

_____

_____

5. How is Moses' greatness shown in his response to God's offer of 32:10?

_____

On what basis did He plead for God's sparing the people? (32:11-13).

_____

6. Justify Moses' anger on seeing what the people had done. What do you learn about sin and its judgment from 32:30-35?

_____

_____

7. What reward did the Levites receive for remaining faithful to God amid the almost universal calf worship? (See Numbers 3:5-10.)

_____

_____

8. What evidences of the people's sorrow for their sin do you find in chapter 33?

_____

_____

9. Note that "tabernacle" is the key word of the paragraph 33:7-11. (Of course, the elaborate Tabernacle of chapters 25-31 had not then been constructed; this was another temporary tabernacle, or "tent of meeting," which Moses hastily built as a place where he and the Israelites might meet God, outside the defiled camp.) What does the tabernacle have to do with the change from "I will not go up in the midst of thee" (33:3) to "My presence shall go with thee" (33:14)?

_____

_____

_____

10. Upon what basis did God renew His fellowship with Israel in chapter 34?

_____

11. What place does the Bible have in the Christian's fellowship with God?

_____

12. Why do you suppose God caused Moses' shining face to be seen by the people?

_____

13. List five important spiritual lessons you have learned from these chapters of Exodus.

_____

_____

_____

II. COMMENTS

A. The Utter Instability, Unreliability, and Wickedness of the Human Heart

Forty days earlier, we left the Israelites encamped around the mountain, worshiping God. The last thing they said to Moses before he started up the mountain was, "All that the Lord hath said will we do, and be obedient" (24:7). Moses had been gone but a short time when they forgot their promise and called upon Aaron to make them gods (32:1), thus violating the very commandment God had emphasized and repeatedly warned them about. What an illustration of the utter instability, unreliability, and wickedness of the human heart! They had set aside His altar, the only means of access; and in its place was the golden calf, the work of their own hands, around which they were shouting and dancing their debasing orgiastic rituals. They had in reality lapsed right back into Egyptian idolatry and abominations. God had been planning a wonderful future for His people. Think how it must have hurt the heart of God that His sacrificial love was spurned.

But in the same manner the professing church in the world today has forgotten God, raised up other idols, and played the harlot. Our great Leader and Deliverer, Christ, has gone to be with God for a time, as did Israel's great leader and deliverer. Moses. Christ has left His church here below to carry out His commands until His return. God is planning a wonderful future for the church as the bride of Christ, to live and reign with Him forever. But how many Christians are faithful stewards? Christ's church has not continued in the way He started it. Many Christians have lapsed into worldliness and sin, ceased to watch for His return, set up idols of their own making, forgotten and broken their vows, and failed to obey the command which He particularly emphasized, "Go ye into all the world, and preach the gospel to every creature" (Mark 16:15).

Many are going through a form of worship and calling it "unto the Lord," but the Lord is not in their thoughts nor in their hearts, and He does not accept such mock worship.

In 1 Corinthians 10:11, referring to the history of Israel, we read, "These things . . . are written for our admonition [learning]." May we indeed learn from them.

B. Aaron's Frailty and Sin

When the people came to Aaron with the frightful proposal of idolatry he, as leader of the people, should have taken a firm stand for the right. If at this critical time he had stood boldly before them; rebuked them for their unbelief; reminded them of God's past goodness; called their attention to the cloud as the manifestation of His presence and the daily-falling manna, which proved that He had not forgotten them; and urged them not to break the very commandment of which God had especially warned them; he might have been able to turn the whole tide of public opinion, saving the nation from this fearful sin. But instead he gave in to the people's demand (32:2-6). Like many leaders of the present day, Aaron did not like their proposition, but he had not the strength of character to withstand them. Notice his weak excuse when Moses charged him with bringing this sin upon the nation (32:21-24). He threw all the blame upon the people and told a falsehood to try and cover his guilt (cf. 32:24; 32:3-4).

C. The Grandeur of Moses' Character

Moses was one of the most remarkable men in all history. This incident in his life brings to the surface several noble traits.

1. *Moses' great opportunity* (32:7-14). Let us go back up the mountain and listen to the conversation between God and Moses (32:7-10). Moses was just about ready to come down. He could not see all that was going on below, but God saw; and, as if to prepare and fortify and perhaps to test His servant, God told him what was taking place and made Moses the offer contained in verse 10. This was the great opportunity of Moses' life for self-advancement. A man less noble would have accepted it, but not Moses.

We have here a glimpse of the greatness of the man as he fell before God in supplication. There was no thought of self. He did not seem to so much as notice the offer that God had made him. God's glory and the people's good were his concerns (see 32:11-13). God has spoken of the people as Moses' people, which he had brought out of Egypt (32:7), but Moses threw them right back on God and called them (v. 11) "thy people which thou hast brought forth."

The three reasons Moses pleaded for sparing the people were: first, they belonged to God; second, it would have brought discredit upon God's name if the people were destroyed (32:12); and third, he remembered God's covenant promise to Abraham, Isaac, and Jacob (32:13). Such powerful pleading caused God to turn from the punishment which the people so fairly deserved (32:14).

2. *Moses' righteous indignation* (32:15-29). So Moses and Joshua (who had been waiting for him further down the mountain) approached the camp. As they came near, the sound of the shouting was heard in the distance, and Joshua, probably remembering the recent fight with Amalek, immediately concluded that it was another war in the camp (v. 17). But Moses knew better and together they hastened forward. As they approached, the whole horrible scene burst upon their view, and Moses, although already

forewarned by God, seemed now to realize for the first time the awful sin of the people. He could not wonder at God's indignation toward them. He cast down the stone tablets on which the law was written, and they lay broken at his feet. The people had broken the law in their hearts; how could they keep it written on stone? Then he rushed in among them, broke up their revelry, took the golden calf, ground it to powder, scattered it upon the water, and made them drink it.

But evidently more heroic measures than this had to be taken to stop this awful wave of idolatry that was threatening to inundate the nation. So Moses, taking his stand in the gate of the camp, demanded, "Who is on the Lord's side?" and all the sons of Levi gathered themselves together unto him. At the command of God, these Levites went throughout the camp administering the sentence of death to about 3,000 men who were found still engaged in idolatrous and immoral rituals.

Moses' zeal for the people when talking with God on the mount now changed into a zeal for God when dealing with the people in the camp. Surely the days in which we are living call for prophets who will not fear to speak for God against sin.

3. *Moses' offer of himself* (32:30-35). Having dealt in judgment, Moses now purposed in selfless love to go and offer himself as a substitute for the people. The atonement he expected to make was the sacrifice of his own life in their stead (32:32). We see the same spirit later in Paul, who was willing to be cut off from Christ if thereby his brethren—his kinsmen according to the flesh—might be saved (Rom. 9:3).

But God did not accept Moses' offer, because Moses could not die as a vicarious substitute for his kinsmen. God said, "Whosoever hath sinned against me, him will I blot out of my book" (32:33). Christ is the only one whose death was vicarious for the sins of mankind, for He was true man, as Son of Man and Head of the human race; and true God, sinless and without blemish. (Read Isa. 53:6; 2 Cor. 5:19-21; 1 Pet. 2:24; John 3:16.)

4. *Moses' fuller knowledge of God* (33:1–34:35). By their sin and stubbornness the people nearly forfeited God's presence among them, and it was only when they humbled themselves and Moses repeatedly pleaded for them that God consented to go with them, as seen in 33:1-17.

Moses requested that God show him His glory (33:18). He wanted a more intimate acquaintance with this mighty God, a greater insight into the glories of His character. God always responds to such a request. He delights to reveal Himself to His children. So He called Moses up alone to the mountain—it is only when we are alone with God that we can become intimately acquainted with Him; and as Moses stood in the cleft of the rock, the afterglow of God's character was revealed to him—His mercy, longsuffering, goodness, truth, and justice (34:5-7). Then, completely overwhelmed, he bowed his head and worshiped, and his one prayer was that God would pardon their iniquity and dwell with them. Could we, as did Moses, catch but a partial glimpse of God's glory, we would see clearly the awful iniquity of man and the necessity for God to pardon before He can dwell among us.

5. *Moses' shining face* (34:29-35). Moses remained on the mountain forty days as before, receiving various instructions from God and writing again the Ten Commandments on tables of stone (34:1-28). When he descended into the camp this time the people were ready to receive him and his messages; but, all unconsciously to Moses, his face shone so that the people were afraid, and he was obliged to put on a veil when he talked with them. Today those who spend time alone with the Lord will surely reflect Him in their faces, and others will see that they have been with the Lord and will listen to their message.

D. The Faithful Few

Read 32:25-28 again and notice that when Moses came down from the mountain and found the people worshiping the golden calf and demanded, "Who is on the Lord's side?" that all the sons of Levi, all Moses' relatives, responded to the call and came and took their stand by Moses.

These Levites apparently had not entered into the calf worship at all but, like Caleb, had wholly followed the Lord. It may have been hard for them to stand against public opinion, hard to refuse to worship the calf when the elders and leaders of Israel, and even Aaron himself, sanctioned it. But later on they received a great reward of the privilege of serving about the Tabernacle for having stood firmly on God's demands.

If our great Leader and Deliverer, Jesus Christ, should suddenly appear in our midst today to break up the idols, rebuke the unfaithful leaders, and demand who is on the Lord's side, would you and I be among the sons of Levi who could take our places on the Lord's side as not having joined in the sin and worldliness which, like a threatening tide, is sweeping into our churches today? Be assured, difficult as it may seem to stand firmly by the old plain truths of the Word of God, that if we are faithful until the end there is a rich reward in store for us.

E. God's People Must Be Separate

God here warns Israel again (34:10-17), as He has done in chapter 23, and as He does repeatedly until they reach Canaan, that they must not, under any circumstances, have friendly relationships with these condemned nations that God said He would drive out of the land. Israel was not to make covenants with them, or to intermarry; and the reason for all this is plain. God called Himself a jealous God (34:14); and knowing how weak and wicked His people were, He wanted them to take every precaution against being led off to the worship of other gods. Thus He insisted upon their observing all the feasts and holy days mentioned in 34:18-26. They were to be so occupied with Jehovah and His worship and work that they would have no time for idols. Human nature is ever the same. God's people today should be totally occupied with Him, His worship, and His work, lest they be led into the worship of idols of the people among whom they live.

III. SUMMARY

Four words summarize the narrative of Exodus 32-34:

> SIN
> JUDGMENT
> INTERCESSION
> RENEWAL

The people's sin was a great sin: spiritual harlotry attended by corrupt abominations. God's judgment was consuming, declared by a jealous Lord. Moses' intercession was desperate, appealing to the mercy of God. And the consequent renewal of fellowship between Israel and God was conditional upon the people's repentance for sin and determination to obey the words of the covenant.

The cycle represented by the four words was a constantly recurring sequence in the history of Israel from this time forward. After coming to the place of renewal, the people would move back to the dwellings of sin again—and the cycle would repeat itself. That Israel was not ever utterly consumed is explained only by the mercy of God and by the ministry of prophets, judges, and men like Moses who pled in behalf of their brethren. That God was pleased to work through His chosen leaders is illustrated in this lesson by the experience of Moses, whose delay on the mountain was the occasion for his people to sin at the beginning of the narrative, but whose presence at the end of the narrative was an occasion of awe and respect—all because Moses spoke for God.

Lesson 12

Tabernacle Construction

When Moses came down from the mountain the first time the people were so engrossed in sin that they were in no condition to hear about the Tabernacle; but now this second time as he returned to them they seemed to be wholly prepared. We have seen in the last lesson some of the experiences they went through that brought about a change of heart, making them ready at last to listen to him. Moses gathered the Israelites around him to tell the wonderful news God had already told him, that God was coming down to dwell among them in a special way, in a tabernacle that they must build.

I. ANALYSIS

First read the six chapters without lingering over the details of the many articles of Tabernacle furniture. Be on the lookout for words and phrases that appear from time to time having explicit spiritual content. Your search for the implied typical truths should come later in your study. Make notations in your Bible as you read.

Study the following outline of these chapters; then reread each paragraph in the Bible text, recording on the chart an identification of the contents of the paragraph (each identification should be no longer than three words).

For review and comparison refer back to your analysis of chapters 25-31 where the specifications of the Tabernacle are recorded.

Now proceed with the following instructions and suggestions for study:

1. Read 35:1–36:7. What relation does the paragraph 35:1-3 have to this PREPARATIONS section?

THE TABERNACLE CONSTRUCTED

35:1	36:8		39:32	40:1	40:34
PREPARATIONS	ITEMS MADE		INSPECTION	TABERNACLE ERECTED	GLORY OF THE LORD
35:1-3	36:8-19	39:1-7	39:32-43	40:1-8	40:34-38
4-19	20-30			9-16	
20-29	31-34	8-21			
35:30—36:1	35-38			17-19	
	37:1-9			20-33	
36:2-7	10:16	22-26			
	17-24				
	25-29	27-29			
	38:1-7				
	8				
	9-20	30-31			
	21-31				

What are the two subjects of 35:4-19?

_____

_____

What spiritual lessons do you learn from 35:20-29 and 36:2-7 concerning offerings to God?

_____

_____

To whom were the offerings made (35:22)?

To whom delivered? (See 36:3.)

2. Read 36:8–39:31. To what does paragraph 38:21-31 refer?

What spiritual lesson may be learned from the fact of great detail in the specifications of the Tabernacle, its furniture, and the priestly garments?

3. Read 39:32-43. As of this time was the Tabernacle itself completed? (v. 32).

What lessons may be learned from verse 43?

4. Read 40:1-33. How does paragraph 40:1-8 differ from 40:17-19?

What is the key word of paragraph 40:9-16? Compare this section with chapter 29.

How does 40:17-19 differ from 40:20-33?

Who is credited with erecting the Tabernacle? (See 40:17-33.)

_____

_____

Why this identification?

_____

Name some perils to which the Israelites might have been exposed during their labors.

_____

_____

5. Read 40:34-38. Contemplate the phrase "glory of the Lord." How is this reference a fitting and climactic conclusion to the book of Exodus?

_____

_____

Contrast the atmosphere of this conclusion with the atmosphere of chapter 1.

_____

_____

In what sense was the cloud a visible manifestation of God dwelling among the Israelites?

_____

According to these verses, what two main activities was the Israelites' day composed of in the wilderness?

_____

_____

6. Make a list of some of the main spiritual lessons learned from these chapters.

_____

_____

_____

_____

7. Referring to the survey chart (p. 9), review your study of the entire book of Exodus and list ten important lessons it teaches.

_____

_____

_____

_____

_____

_____

II. COMMENTS

A. The Willing-hearted

Moses told the Israelites at the very outset (35:4-5) that he wanted only those with willing heart to contribute to the building—just as God would have only the willing ones contribute now to the edification of His church (Eph. 2:21-22; 2 Cor. 8:12; 9:6-7).

When Moses had finished giving the list of materials which would be needed in the construction (35:5-19), everyone whose "heart stirred him up, and everyone whom his spirit made willing," went and brought something to help in the work and presented it, not to Moses, but unto the Lord (35:20-22, 29).

B. Giving What They Had

Notice that everyone brought offerings of just what he or she happened to have (see 35:23-25, 27). The rulers who had precious stones brought them (v. 27). The men who had only wood brought that (v. 24). Those who had ram skins or badger skins brought them, and the women brought linen and stuff that they had spun. It was as though they had gone to their tents and taken an inventory of their belongings and had given to the Lord whatever could be used. We do not hear of anyone's refusing to contribute the piece of acacia wood or fine linen he did have just because he had no costly precious stones. The wood and the linen were just as necessary as the precious stones. Valuable practical lessons may be learned from this. In the building of His church God needs various kinds of materials, and He wants just what each individual has, not what he has not. Everyone has something that can be used. Let us each take an inventory and see what it is. Some have money, others education, a talent in one direction or another, time, influence—all are needed in this great work and nothing should be withheld. We do not read in the text of Moses having to preach any sermons on the duty of giving in order to stir the people to liberality. Neither do we read of their planning any bazaars or entertainment to raise the necessary funds. Nor do we read of any subscription paper passed around among the Amalekites or other heathen tribes asking them to contribute; and there is no mention of a Tabernacle debt. On the contrary, the gifts came in such abundance that it became necessary for Moses to send out a command that no more offerings be brought, and the people were *restrained* from giving! (36:5-7).

Has such a restraint ever been duplicated in the history of the church? Yet it is a carefully studied estimate that if each professing Christian in America were to give even one-tenth of his income yearly, the Lord's treasuries for both home and foreign work would be literally overflowing. What is lacking? Is there not something wrong that such difficulty is experienced regarding the finances for God's work? We should not like to think that those Israelites, living long ago under law and who had just recently turned their backs to God and worshiped idols, loved their God more than we do—we who are living in this glorious dispensation of grace, so much nearer to the coming of the King. We must remember that the cost of the Tabernacle was no small amount for that fugitive nation to raise, but their enthusiastic joy that the Lord was coming to dwell with them as soon as they got His dwelling place ready made them regard lightly all expense and labor. If we lived more in the constant expectation of His coming would we not be more diligent and liberal?

There are many things in the Israelites' experiences that we should seek to avoid, but their ready response to God's demand and their worshiping Him with their substance we would do well to imitate.

C. Obedience and God's Approval

If we compare the account of the construction of the Tabernacle (chaps. 36-39) with the instructions given to Moses (chaps. 25-31) we observe that they correspond accurately. All things were done in accordance with the pattern shown to Moses on the mount.

When the workmen had finished making the parts of the Tabernacle they brought everything to Moses (39:32-43); and Moses set up the Tabernacle just a year after they started from Egypt (see 40:17). He carefully assembled every piece as directed, each article of furniture in its exact position (see 40:18-33). When all was done a wonderful thing took place: God came down and filled the

Tabernacle with His glory (40:34-35). He had kept His word given in Exodus 25:8, and from that time on He would speak to them not from the fiery Mount Sinai, but from between the cherubim above the mercy seat within the Tabernacle (see Lev. 1:1).

D. Other Notes

1. *The cost of the Tabernacle.* This staggers one's imagination. Read 38:24-25 and also 35:5-19 and estimate for yourself the enormous expenditure made. "No money had been coined; it had to be weighed. Actual values of gold and silver can be estimated only approximately. Classically, a talent of gold equaled $13,800 and a talent of silver $538; a shekel of gold $8 and a shekel of silver 50 cents. One standard of values remains—a day's wages and what can be bought for it; but monetary wages are not mentioned in our early Scriptures."[1] One thing we know, that the Tabernacle represented an enormous expenditure and served as a monument to the people's gratitude to God. "It is significant that the Tabernacle rested upon, and its curtains were hung upon the silver that was the representative contribution of every man in the congregation of Israel. The Tabernacle stood thus upon the dedication of God's redeemed people."[2]

2. *The cloud.* A miraculous pillar, indicating God's presence, governed the movements of the Israelites (Ex. 40:36-37; Num. 9:15-23). This cloud, spreading over them and protecting them from the burning sun, became a fire by night to give light (Ps. 105:39). Jehovah Himself was in the pillar (see Ex. 13:21), so it was He Himself who controlled the movements of the people. God's people today should be just as absolutely under His control.

3. *Inspiration.* One proof of the inspiration of the Scriptures is the testimony of the Bible to itself. C. I. Scofield writes: "The writers affirm, where they speak of the subject at all, that they speak by direct divine authority. (Example, Ezek. 13:1, 13, 20; 14:2, 12; 15:1; 16:1). They invariably testify that the *words*, and not the ideas merely, are inspired. This, of necessity, refers to the original documents, not to translations and versions; but the labors of competent scholars have brought our English versions to a degree of perfection so remarkable that we may confidently rest upon them as authoritative. For example, 1 Corinthians 2:9-14 gives this process by which a truth passes from the mind of God to the

1. Gerrit Verkuyl, ed. *The Holy Bible, The Berkeley Version* (Grand Rapids: Zondervan, 1959), p. 93, n.
2. Charles F. Pfeiffer and Everett F. Harrison, eds., *The Wycliffe Bible Commentary* (Chicago: Moody, 1962), p. 85.

minds of His people: (a) The unseen things of God are undiscoverable by the natural man (v. 9). (b) These unseen things God has revealed to chosen men (vv. 10-12). (c) The revealed things are communicated in Spirit-taught words (v. 13). This implies neither mechanical dictation nor the effacement of the writer's personality, but only that the Spirit infallibly guides in the choice of words from the writer's own vocabulary (v. 13). (d) These Spirit-taught words, in which the revelation has been expressed, are discerned, as to their true spiritual content, only by the spiritual among believers (1 Cor. 2:15-16)." See also 2 Peter 1:20-21 and 2 Timothy 3:16.

Notice in the book of Exodus how often the term "words" appears (i.e., *God's* words). See 4:15, 28, 30; (17:14); 19:6-7; 20:1; 24:3-4, (7), 8, (12); (32:16); 34:1, 28; 35:1.

III. SUMMARY OF THE BOOK OF EXODUS

Exodus, the book of redemption, begins with the Israelites in bondage to Pharaoh, driven by taskmasters, and fearful of death. The book ends with the Israelites delivered from bondage, brought out of Egypt, dwelling safely with their great God in their midst, having their need supplied by Him, and looking forward to a glorious future. Their former groan has been swallowed up in the Lord's glory.

In the opening chapter of Exodus, the pressing need of the people is deliverance; in the closing chapters, the need is that of fellowship—fellowship with God for assurance, sustenance, and protection. To provide for all three, God gave the law for their living, the Tabernacle for their worship, and the wilderness experiences for their testing. In all, He proved Himself the gracious Redeemer; and He continues to so manifest Himself to Christians today.

Bibliography

SELECTED SOURCES FOR FURTHER STUDY

Archer, Gleason L. *A Survey of Old Testament Introduction*. Chicago: Moody, 1964.

Connell, J. C. "Exodus." In *The New Bible Commentary*, edited by F. Davidson, Grand Rapids: Eerdmans, 1953.

Fairbairn, Patrick. *The Typology of Scripture*. Reprint. Grand Rapids: Zondervan, n.d.

Johnson, Philip C. "Exodus." In *The Wycliffe Bible Commentary*, ed. Charles F. Pfeiffer and Everett F. Harrison. Chicago: Moody, 1962.

Manley, G. T. *The New Bible Handbook*. Chicago: InterVarsity, 1950.

Martin, W. S., and Marshall, A. *Tabernacle Types and Teachings*. London: Pickering & Inglis, n.d.

Moorehead, W. G. *Studies in the Mosaic Institutions*. Westwood, N.J.: Revell, 1893.

Morgan, G. Campbell. *The Ten Commandments*. Westwood, N.J.: Revell, 1901.

Payne, J. Barton. *An Outline of Hebrew History*. Grand Rapids: Baker, 1964.

Pfeiffer, Charles, and Vos, Howard. *The Wycliffe Historical Geography of Bible Lands*. Chicago: Moody, 1967.

Pink, Arthur W. *Gleanings in Exodus*. Chicago: Moody, 1962.

Sauer, Erich. *The Dawn of World Redemption*. Grand Rapids: Eerdmans, 1953.

Soltau, Henry W. *The Tabernacle*. Reprint. Fincastle, Va.: Scripture Truth, n.d.

Spink, James F. *Types and Shadows of Christ in the Tabernacle*. New York: Loizeaux, 1946.

Strong, James. *The Tabernacle of Israel.* Reprint. Grand Rapids: Baker, 1952.

Tenney, Merrill C., ed. *The Zondervan Pictorial Bible Dictionary.* Grand Rapids: Zondervan, 1963.

Unger, Merrill F. *Introductory Guide to the Old Testament.* Grand Rapids: Zondervan, 1951.

_____. *Unger's Bible Dictionary.* Chicago: Moody, 1957.

Wood, Leon. *A Survey of Israel's History.* Grand Rapids: Zondervan, 1970.

Young, Edward J. *An Introduction to the Old Testament.* Grand Rapids: Eerdmans, 1949.